The Explicit of Teaching Reading

Joelie Hancock

Editor

The Flinders University of South Australia
Adelaide, South Australia
Australia

International Reading Association
800 Barksdale Road, PO Box 8139
Newark, Delaware 19714-8139, USA
www.reading.org

The International Reading Association attempts, through its publications, to provide a forum for a wide spectrum of opinions on reading. This policy permits divergent viewpoints without implying the endorsement of the Association.

Director of Publications   Joan M. Irwin
Assistant Director of Publications   Jeanette K. Moss
Editor in Chief, Books   Matthew W. Baker
Permissions Editor   Janet S. Parrack
Associate Editor   Tori Mello
Acquisitions and Communications Coordinator   Amy T. Roff
Assistant Editor   Sarah Rutigliano
Publications Coordinator   Beth Doughty
Association Editor   David K. Roberts
Production Department Manager   Iona Sauscermen
Art Director   Boni Nash
Electronic Publishing Supervisor   Wendy A. Mazur
Electronic Publishing Specialist   Anette Schütz-Ruff
Electronic Publishing Specialist   Cheryl J. Strum
Electronic Publishing Assistant   Peggy Mason

Project Editor   Janet S. Parrack

Library of Congress Cataloging in Publication Data
  The explicit teaching of reading / Joelie Hancock, editor.
      p.   cm.
  Includes bibliographical references and index.
  1. Reading.   2. Literacy—social aspects.   1. Hancock, Joelie.   II. International Reading Association.
LB1573.E96   1999   99-39695
372.41'6—dc21
ISBN 0-87207-253-3

Second Printing, April 2001

Contents

Preface   vi

Chapter One   **An Introduction to the Explicit Teaching**   I
                 of Reading
                 Lyn Wilkinson

Chapter Two   **"It's Just a Different Answer"**:   13
                 Exploring Point of View
                 Judy Smith

Chapter Three **Not Just Onions! Exploring Layers**   29
                 of Meaning in Texts
                 Lynda Matthews

Chapter Four   **Building on Cultural Capital: Linking Home**   39
                 and School Literacies With Popular Texts
                 Lyn Shepherd

Chapter Five   **Explicit Processes and Strategies**   49
                 Using Literature Circles
                 Sally Ahang

Chapter Six   **What's Happening in Your**   62
                 Reading Program?
                 Kerry Gehling

Chapter Seven   **The Aim Is Metacognition:**   80
                 For Teachers as Well as Students
                 Meredith Edwards

Chapter Eight   **Explicitly Teaching the Reading**   97
                 of Nonfiction Texts
                 Jay Marshall

Chapter Nine   **But What Do We Make Explicit?**   112
                 Betty Weeks

Afterword   **Reflections on a Teacher Research Group:**   126
                 A Leap Forward
                 Joelie Hancock

Index   131

Contributors

Editor

Joelie Hancock
Senior Lecturer in Education
School of Education
The Flinders University of South Australia
Adelaide, South Australia

Authors

Sally Ahang
Upper Primary School Teacher
Direk Primary School
Salisbury North, South Australia

Meredith Edwards
Assistant Principal
Woodville High School
Woodville, South Australia

Kerry Gehling
Classroom Teacher
Highgate Primary School
Highgate, South Australia

Jay Marshall
Learning Support and Literacy Teacher
Woodcroft College
Morphett Vale, South Australia

Lynda Matthews
Project Officer, Early Assistance
Department of Education,
    Training and Employment
Adelaide, South Australia

Lyn Shepherd
Classroom Teacher
Department for Education and
    Children's Services
Salisbury North, South Australia

Judy Smith
Classroom Teacher
Westbourne Park Primary School
Daw Park, South Australia

Betty Weeks
Classroom Teacher
Flaxmill Primary School
Morphett Vale, South Australia

Lyn Wilkinson
Lecturer in Education
The Flinders University of South
    Australia
Adelaide, South Australia

v

Preface

The teachers in this book came together to explore the explicit teaching of reading at the beginning of 1997. They had identified an aspect of their reading program that they wanted to improve by "being more explicit" and agreed to meet once a month on Saturday mornings to share and clarify their concerns, their plans, and their teaching. The group was supported by funding from the South Australian ESL and Child Literacy Research Node, and I was the research mentor. I had two purposes: to support the research for the node, and to help the teachers prepare and present their classroom findings at a professional development Saturday, organized by the Adelaide Council of the Australian Literacy Educators' Association (ALEA), formerly an Australian Reading Association council. After their presentations the teacher-researchers decided to write up their work.

The Saturday ALEA program had been planned to meet concerns of South Australian teachers about how to teach reading explicitly. Early literacy teachers in the state had become familiar with *explicit teaching* because of the strong emphasis it was given in a South Australian *Cornerstones* (1996) inservice course that many of them had attended. That course, developed and conducted across the state, raised a number of issues about the learning needs of children, particularly those from different sociocultural backgrounds. One of those issues was for teachers to be clear about what they wanted and expected from students: to be "explicit."

What Is Explicit Teaching?

Spelling out aspects of literacy learning clearly is supported by a number of different theories and related practices, which include (1) those concerned with developing independent, strategic readers (Paris, Wixson, & Palincsar, 1986); (2) the breaking of learning into small, discrete, and carefully taught steps (Westwood, 1995); (3) the so-called "genre approach" to writing (Comber & Cormack, 1995); and (4) the need to demystify literacy processes and purposes for nonmainstream students (Freebody, Ludwig, & Gunn, 1995). These four concerns and emphases in literacy teaching have been influencial throughout Australia over the last 15 years. However, *explicit teaching* did not become a common term among teachers until they were introduced to helping students articulate and list the structures and features of different text types as part of the genre approach to writing.

Too often in classrooms, many students are left guessing how they should behave and what they should do to become successful readers and writers. Sometimes this is because teachers themselves are not clear about what students should do to learn; sometimes it is because teachers have not seen any advantage in explaining the purposes, processes, and outcomes to the learners; and sometimes it is because teachers have not realized that their talk and their modelling has confused rather than enlightened their learners. This classroom confusion has been documented by Delpit (1988) in the United States and has been termed *interactive trouble* by Freebody et al. (1995) in their study of early literacy classrooms in Australia. As teachers accept their responsibility in reducing students' confusion about literacy learning, they are being challenged to look more closely at the processes of learning, and to be more precise in their teaching.

About This Book

This book is the result of a group of teachers who took a closer look at their teaching so that they could be clearer to their students.

Chapter 1 is based on a presentation by Lyn Wilkinson at the Saturday inservice on explicit teaching. Wilkinson explains how explicit teaching was originally advocated to improve the learning of text structures and features by students whose home and community literacies did not include texts necessary for success in the broader society. She associates explicit teaching with teaching secondary discourses (Gee, 1990) and with students gaining insights into language and its uses through metacognition. She explains that explicit teaching is not a panacea for poor literacy performance, and she spells out the dangers of overusing this type of teaching.

The next eight chapters are by teacher-researchers, who teach classes from the first year of school, which children enter at the age of 5, through Year 8, which is the first year of secondary school in South Australia. Each author gives an account of the significant insights gained, and each examines a different aspect of her reading program.

In Chapter 2, Judy Smith writes about improving her teaching of point of view. She has found that when asked for their point of view, her school beginners need to tune into their own sensory experiences and interpretations and not be influenced by the teacher's or other children's suggestions. By recording the students' opinions and perceptions in a large book that the class could revisit and by awarding stars to students who did follow their own perceptions, she was able to make progress in this aspect of her teaching.

Lynda Matthews wanted to improve students' text analysis. In Chapter 3, she explores the layers of meaning in stories with her combined Years 1 and 2 class. Many aspects of her teaching contribute to her success and the students' enjoyment of this exploration. She has concluded that her students' engagement in their learning is due to the classroom climate of student ownership where all students contribute and feel successful; to her commitment to involving parents in their children's learning; to the students catching on to *top story* and *bottom story* when talking of layers of meaning; and to her practice of thinking and reflecting out loud. No doubt the appeal of the books she has chosen—mostly by Margaret Wild—also has something to do with it.

In Chapter 4, Lyn Shepherd tackles the teaching of reading in her Years 2 and 3 class. She had found herself working in a number of areas. First, she had discovered whether the texts she uses in her classroom are different from those that the children read at home. Second, she had made it obvious to the children that she and the school value the home texts by making them a focus for a unit of work and an ongoing part of the class reading program. Third, she made clear the elements of a magazine by brainstorming these elements with the children and then charting them, by using these elements to label baskets in the classroom publishing workshop, and by referring to the chart and the basket labels as the children prepare their magazine contributions.

It did not take Sally Ahang long to discover that her Years 6 and 7 students needed to read more actively and respond to what they read more critically and thoughtfully. In Chapter 5, she describes her reading and what led her to a teaching strategy using literature circles. With a clear goal and a broad strategy in mind, she clarified her expectations and the students' learning activities by determining (1) four student outcomes that she would aim for, (2) exactly what would show her she was achieving these outcomes, and (3) what support she could provide that would make clear what she wanted and remind her students what they were required to do. The support she provided included proformas that structured the students' recording of their book preferences, what the students did each day in literature circles, how the students were to act in their groups and what she would observe, how to structure their paragraphs of response, and the options they could choose for their follow-up activities. In very concrete ways Ahang made explicit to herself and her students what aspects of reading she wanted to teach and how her goals would be accomplished.

In Chapter 6, Kerry Gehling tells how a parent's dissatisfaction with her child's reading program motivated her to make more explicit to all parents the goals and learning activities of her Years 6 and 7 reading program. She believed that because her reading goals were not those expected by the parents, they were not recognized and therefore not appreciated. A letter to parents at the beginning of the term described exactly what the students would be learning about information texts, about diagrams, and about reading with expression. Assessment proformas also informed students and parents what the activities were aiming for and achieving. After the unit of work was completed, a letter was sent to parents asking them how well they understood the intended outcomes of the class reading program and whether the program met their expectations of what their child should be taught in school.

Meredith Edwards, coordinator in a secondary school, was resourceful in finding funding and professional development expertise to support the Year 8 English and society and environment teachers as they explored strategies that would improve their students' reading and identified teaching strategies that would support the students' learning of these strategies. The model presented in Chapter 7 that spelled out before-reading, during-reading, and after-reading strategies gave the teachers something concrete to hand out and explain to students, to refer to as students tackled particular texts, and to use in providing feedback to students. In working together on improving their students' reading, teachers benefitted from shared understandings and common language.

As a literacy coordinator in a secondary school, Jay Marshall recognized that explicit teaching includes providing models, frameworks, a clear progression of steps, listed criteria, and written feedback that refers to these frameworks. She also knew that these spelled-out strategies and procedures work best if they build on what the students already know; if teachers have ways of finding out what their students are finding helpful; and if teachers work together to understand teaching strategies, support students with the same set of strategies, and provide consistent feedback on these strategies. In Chapter 8, Marshall describes a set of reading strategies that she and a coteacher taught as part of a research unit on Greece.

In Chapter 9, Betty Weeks refers to Freebody and Luke's (1990) model of a literacy user, which points out the different aspects of being a reader and writer. This model identifies four roles of a literacy user: code-breaker, text participant, text user, and text analyst. Weeks shows how teachers can make explicit what is involved in each role, by describing a research unit of learning and by highlighting the different aspects of reading that a teacher can make explicit throughout the unit.

In the Afterword, I summarize the research process that has helped teachers to try new strategies and to reflect on the strategies' effects. The research was a way for the teachers to spend extra time planning and reflecting on their teaching, and to express their plans and reflections through talking and writing. The teachers gained in a number of ways by being explicit to themselves, to each other, and to their students. Their teaching was more purposeful and focused. Teachers felt more confident and articulate in their schools as professionals, they felt more part of a broader professional community, and they saw an increase in their students' engagement in learning and in their learning outcomes.

The accounts in these chapters reveal the complexities of teaching reading and the many ways that teachers can plan to make their teaching more explicit. Putting expectations into words is an important part of being explicit, and written plans, charts, proformas, written guides, listed criteria, and labels make these words concrete. But before teachers can put into words what they expect students to do and understand, teachers must be clear themselves about exactly what they want to achieve. Reading and hearing about other teachers' practices, talking about them, and reaching a common understanding and language have been crucial aspects of these teachers' successes in teaching reading explicitly.

Joelie Hancock

References

Comber, B., & Cormack, P. (1995). Analyzing early literacy teaching practices. In *Cornerstones* (Appendix 1, Module 4). Adelaide, SA: Department of Education and Children's Services.

Cornerstones: Training and development program. (1996). Adelaide, SA: Department of Education and Children's Services.

Delpit, L. (1988). The silenced dialogue: Power and pedagogy in educating other people's children. *Harvard Educational Review, 58*, 280–298.

Freebody, P., Ludwig, C., & Gunn, S. (1995). Everyday literacy practices in and out of schools. In *Children's Literacy National Project* (Vol. 1, pp. 297–315). Adelaide, SA: Department of Education, Employment, and Training.

Freebody, P., & Luke, A. (1990). Literacies' programs: Debates and demands in a cultural context. *Prospect: Journal of Adult Migrant Education Programs, 5*(3), 7–16.

Gee, J. (1990). *Social linguistics and literacy: Ideology in discourses*. Basingstoke, UK: Falmer Press.

Paris, S., Wixson, K., & Palincsar, A. (1986). Instructional approaches to reading comprehension. In E. Rothkopf (Ed.), *Review of research in education*. Washington, DC: American Educational Research Association.

Westwood, P. (1995). What should we be teaching explicitly to at-risk beginning readers and writers? In *Cornerstones* (Modules 6 and 7, pp. 54–57). Adelaide, SA: Department of Education and Children's Services.

Chapter One

An Introduction to the Explicit Teaching of Reading

Lyn Wilkinson

Lyn Wilkinson is a lecturer in Language and Literacy at Flinders University, South Australia. Since writing a paper in 1995 on explicit teaching for *Cornerstones*, a professional development program for teachers of early literacy, she has been seeking a literacy-learning model that can explain the place of explicit teaching in students' learning. In this chapter she describes how James Gee's notion of discourse and his distinction between two ways of learning accommodate both explicit teaching and whole language teaching. In addition, these ideas explain how explicit teaching is particularly appropriate for nonmainstream students and how it leads to the development of metacognition.

In Western capitalist societies, which are experiencing "a speedy, ruthless transition from an industrial to an information-based economy" (Stuckey, 1991, p. viii), literacy skills are seen to be an integral part of our identities as people, workers, and citizens. Our personal *literacy sets* (the ways in which we are able to draw on the variety of competencies within our literacy repertoire in order to achieve different purposes in a variety of contents) play a large part in determining our status in society, our job opportunities, our income, and our ability to manage our lives. Literacy has become commodified—a saleable resource.

Because literacy is seen to be so intricately linked to personal identity, social status, and power, in times of "large-scale social, cultural, and economic change" (Comber, Green, Lingard, & Luke, 1998, p. 22), attention often turns to the literacy achievements of students and young people (Green, Hodgens, & Luke, 1997). It is therefore not surprising, given the world economic crisis, that in the last few years there have been increasingly strident calls from politicians, the media, and the general public for schools to "get back to the basics," in the erroneous belief that improving students' literacy will somehow magically improve the unemployment statistics. Simultaneously, educators and educational researchers have been concerned about social justice issues, in particular, the failure of large groups of students from disadvantaged and diverse communities to improve their literacy scores on standardized measures of achievement and to move into the kinds of employment that bring status and financial reward. They may be fueled by different imperatives, but both these discourses have encouraged educators to examine the literacy curriculum offered in schools and the pedagogy through which it is delivered.

One of the terms that has been used with increased frequency in discussions about literacy and literacy pedagogy is *explicit teaching*. Explicit teaching came to the foreground in Australia in the mid-1980s after educational linguists including Frances Christie, Jim Martin, and Joan Rothery developed what has come to be called the "genre approach" to teaching writing (see White & Young, 1989). These educational researchers were concerned that school curricula at that time did not give students from disadvantaged and diverse communities access to the kinds of literacies that they claimed are associated with power in our society. The same kinds of concerns were raised in the United States, where, for example, Delpit (1998) argued that although whole language classroom pedagogy gave students access to personal literacy, it was not an appropriate approach for teaching power-code literacy.

Teachers who were concerned about achieving better literacy outcomes for students from disadvantaged and targeted groups (Aboriginals, and low-income ESL, disabled, and female students) embraced a pedagogy that identified the genres (reports, arguments, and other kinds of persuasive writing and expositions) deemed powerful in our society. Teachers explicitly taught students to analyze, name, and reproduce the linguistic structures and features of the more common forms of these genres. They did this believing that literacy outcomes would be enhanced as students learned to understand and use these powerful genres for themselves.

Given the connections between language and power, why should explicit teaching about aspects of language be restricted to writing? If student access to the language of power in written form is enhanced through explicit teaching of aspects of genre, then it follows that explicit teaching across the literacy curriculum—including reading—will make a significant difference for students whose home and community literacies are not those that are valued most by the wider society. Explicit teaching can reveal to these students the particular kinds of language that count when it comes to achieving both school success and social advancement.

But explicit teaching alone will not make a significant difference in literacy outcomes for students from disadvantaged and targeted groups, because educational outcomes are constructed largely by wider social forces (Comber et al., 1998; Connell, 1992, 1993; Connell, Johnston, & White, 1994; Eveline, 1994; Stuckey, 1991) that lie outside the control of the classroom teacher. And herein lies the rub for teachers: Explicit teaching gives students access to many aspects of literacy, both information and ways of operating, that can make a difference for them, but it is not a panacea for disadvantage or a sure-fire way of fixing the problem. Without explicit teaching, many students will not gain the information and ways of operating they need to act powerfully in the world. Even with explicit teaching, however, there is no guarantee that their measured literacy outcomes will improve. Students should not be denied access to knowledge and ways of operating that will allow them to better understand and shape their world, nor should they be led to believe that if they master the forms and language of power their life outcomes will be better.

Subconscious Acquisition and Conscious Learning

James Gee's (1990) discussion of acquired and learned *discourses* further illuminates the task for teachers of students from disadvantaged and targeted groups. Gee argues that language is a communicative act embedded in social interactions, and that in order to understand language we need not focus on language itself but on discourses: "ways of being in the world, or forms of life which integrate words, acts, values, beliefs, attitudes, social identities, as well as gestures, glances, body positions, and clothes" (p. 142). Gee identifies two kinds of discourses:

- *primary discourses*, which are acquired "subconsciously by exposure to models," and
- *secondary discourses*, which are learned consciously, either "through teaching…or through certain life experiences that trigger conscious reflection." (p. 146)

The acquisition of mother-tongue oral language (primary discourse) is closely tied to the present, to the material world, and to immediate and concrete experiences. Initial oral-language acquisition occurs in highly purposeful contexts in which function is readily apparent. Generally, this is not the case with reading and writing (secondary discourses), which need to be learned and which will benefit from explicit teaching. Gee (1990) argues that

All school activities, and thus all literacy activities, are bound to particular Discourses. There is no such thing as "reading" or "writing," only reading or writing something (a text of a certain type) in a certain way with certain values…. We read and write only within a Discourse, never outside all of them. (p. xviii)

That is, he constructs literacy (or more accurately literacies, because there are so many manifestations) as a sociocultural phenomenon, which invites us to understand it in ways that are different from the psycholinguistic view of reading that has predominated for many years. The sociocultural view of literacies is significant because it exposes the myth of "the level playing field" and allows teachers to understand literacy failure in ways that do not promote a deficit view of certain cultural and ethnic groups in our society (Badger & Wilkinson, 1999).

Schools promote, teach, and assess certain valued literacies and reward students' mastery of them. Students who behave and speak in certain ways in the classroom, enjoy particular kinds of texts, reveal their understandings in specific ways, and demonstrate mastery of the forms of speaking and writing that are valued by the mandated curriculum, are perceived to be successful. Students who do not display these traits are judged as being less able, perhaps even as being deficient. This differential performance comes about because school discourses are closer to those discourses used in some students' homes and families than in others. That is, for some groups of students there is more similarity between what Gee calls the primary discourses of home and family and the secondary discourses taught at school. Viewed from this perspective, success is not about individual effort but rather the match between students' existing literacies and those taught by the school.

In the late 1980s, the influence of researchers who promoted literacy pedagogies that called for more emphasis on acquisition (for example, Cambourne, 1988; Goodman, 1986; Holdaway, 1979) became very strong in Australian schools. In many instances, the effect of what subsequently became known as the whole language movement was positive. Children's increasing enjoyment of reading and writing as they devoured trade books, chose their own topics, and wrote for real audiences became evident. There was lively engagement in classroom literacy events, which many educators would argue had not been the case with basal readers, isolated phonics instruction, and the weekly teacher-set composition.

However, the work of whole language advocates ignored the fact that school literacies are mainly secondary discourses, and that students therefore need to learn how to do them. For example, students need to learn the discourse expected at school when picture books are read to them: to allow the adult to handle the book, to listen without interrupting, to differentiate between the actual reading and teacher invitations to respond to the text, to choose appropriate responses to the text, to sit in particular ways in designated places, and to indicate through body language that they are listening. Some students' primary discourse, acquired in their homes, allows them to be immediately successful in this situation. For them there is a continuum from the primary to the secondary discourse (often the explicit teaching associated with the learning of secondary discourses has already begun). But for other students there is a severe disjunction between their home discourse around texts and reading and that expected by the school. These students are then judged as less successful, problematic, deficient, or in need of remediation. The locus of the problem becomes the student rather than the school curriculum or the classroom pedagogy (Alloway & Gilbert, 1998, p. 254).

Learning secondary discourses, of which print literacies are a part, requires explanation, analysis, and the development of metaknowledge. That is, explicit teaching is not only appropriate but essential if all students are to become successful. Gee (1990) claims that "we are better at performing what we acquire, but we consciously know more about what we have learned...acquisition is good for performance, learning is good for meta-level knowledge" (p. 146). This is why, if it is to be of maximum benefit to students from disadvantaged and targeted groups, explicit teaching must be embedded in a particular kind of pedagogy, where pedagogy refers in a holistic sense to the eclectic sum of the methodologies used within a classroom.

Explicit teaching is largely about giving students access to those aspects of school literacies that result in successful outcomes as measured by school and state assessment procedures. But unless there are opportunities for subconscious acquisition through exposure to models as well as use of the discourse in meaningful social contexts, these students are unlikely to become proficient performers within the discourse; they will inadvertently reveal themselves as "outsiders." They may know about the discourse, but may not be able to demonstrate the same proficiency in using it as other students. One of the reasons for this is that any discourse is a complex way of saying–doing–thinking–feeling–valuing (Gee, 1990, p. xv). This complexity is such that it is impossible for teachers to separate all the component parts and teach them explicitly. For example, in essay writing students can be taught explicitly different ways of structuring an essay (e.g., Clyne, 1996), use of active and passive constructions, cohesive features, the different kinds of connectives (temporal, causal, and contrastive) that act as markers for the reader, and linguistic devices like nominalization and modality (Halliday, 1994). But it is extremely difficult to teach explicitly elements like style and tone, even though these count in English assessments of students in the final year of secondary school (Freebody, 1992). Freebody asserts that because of

> the *increased competence* of the candidature...the criteria that need to be called increasingly into play in order to discriminate among students become increasingly difficult to specify, and come thus to be based largely on displays of cultural sophistication—displays that are difficult if not impossible to teach in any explicit manner. (p. 96)

If we want to make a difference for students whose primary discourses (home and community literacy practices) are significantly different from secondary discourses (school literacy practices), then explicit teaching must be embedded within a classroom pedagogy in which both acquisition and learning are made possible. As Gee (1990) notes,

> [a]cquisition and learning are differential sources of power: acquirers usually beat learners at performance, learners usually beat acquirers at talking about it, that is, at explication, explanation, analysis and criticism. (p. 146)

Because proficiency in both areas is rewarded by the school assessment system, students need to develop their abilities as performers within school discourses, as well as their ability to explain, analyze, and critique. The initial emphasis in the classroom must be on acquisition because

> learning can facilitate nothing unless the acquisition process has already begun. You cannot overtly teach anyone a discourse, in a classroom or anywhere else. This is not to say that acquisition cannot go on in a classroom, but only that if it does, this isn't because of overt "teaching," but because of a process of "apprenticeship" and social practice. Acquisition must (at least partially) precede learning; apprenticeship must precede "teaching".... Classrooms that do not properly balance acquisition and learning, and realize which is which, and which student has acquired what, simply privilege those students who have begun the acquisition process at home, engaging these students in a teaching/learning process, while the others simply "fail." (Gee, 1990, p. 147)

Au (cited in Freppon & Dahl, 1998) puts it another way:

> I am convinced that we cannot be successful with these students (from diverse backgrounds) if they do not first see the reason for becoming literate. First, they must fall in love with books and, as Lucy Calkins puts it, they must write from the heart. Then they can see the point of skill instruction. (p. 242)

In this respect the whole language movement has it right. Students need to be immersed in school discourses about literacy because it is only as they begin to acquire them, which also means appreciating and understanding their social function, that explicit teaching will have the desired outcomes.

The current plea from literacy educators for a "balanced curriculum" (see Freppon & Dahl, 1998), which combines elements of whole language teaching with more explicit and focused learning about the component parts of language (phonics, grammatical structure, and genre), mirrors what is advocated here. Gee's work offers a powerful theoretical understanding of why we need a balanced curriculum. Acquisition and learning achieve different ends, and both are needed if students are to become competent in literacy performance and develop skills like analysis and critique, which require metalevel knowledge. Teachers who understand the need for balance are in a position to make significant curriculum and pedagogical decisions, which can make a difference to the outcomes of students from disadvantaged and targeted groups.

The classroom emphasis on either "acquisition via immersion and demonstration" or "learning via explicit teaching" will change from lesson to lesson according to students' needs. Immersion in literature and storytelling and demonstrations of different kinds of literacies by experienced users will support acquisition of fluent performance. Explicit teaching will assist students in focusing on particular aspects of literacy and learning the metalevel skills and understandings that allow for analysis, explanation, and critique.

The Place of Metacognition in Explicit Teaching

One of the goals of explicit teaching is the development of metacognition—the ability to think and talk about learning or the ability to deal with learning in an abstract way. It is metacognitive ability that allows learners to transfer known information and strategies to new situations, to plan and operate strategically when they are confronted by new learning contexts, and to monitor and evaluate their attempts and adjust behavior when they are less successful than they would wish. The teacher who uses explicit methods deliberately provides insights into the ways in which a proficient language user operates, encouraging students to be aware of their own processes and giving them the language to talk about it. In part, the explicit teaching of reading is about making the hidden obvious; about exposing and explaining what is taken for granted; about demystifying mental processes; about bringing embedded ideas, values, and cultural norms to the surface; and about letting children in on the information and strategies that will enable them to become powerful literacy users.

The teaching of reading has become much more than phonics and comprehension. For example, reading a picture book may require students to identify mood using color clues in the illustrations, to understand that text and illustrations may each carry a different storyline thus creating tension or humor, to make inferences about a character's motives from the dialogue, to recognize nuance and irony, to understand how intertextual cues convey humor, to appreciate metaphor, or to recognize parody. Teaching reading means supporting students as they learn how to

- decode texts,
- use existing knowledge to make sense of texts,
- use the text purposefully, and
- recognize the sociocultural values inherent in the text and the way in which the text positions them as a reader. (Based on Freebody & Luke, 1990) (See Chapter 9, p. 124)

Within a classroom literacy pedagogy, teachers can and should explicitly teach each of these four aspects of reading. Teachers can give students access to the information that is required for decoding including graphophonic relationships, print and layout conventions, syntactic structures, and lexical relationships. Teachers can help students to focus on and talk about strategies for making sense of text by articulating how they use syntactic, semantic, and cultural information to make sense of the text, and encouraging students to do the same. Teachers can make explicit the different ways in which texts like timetables, posters, magazines, newspapers, shopping lists, greeting cards, lab reports, and novels are read according to their function and intended audience. Teachers can use explicit teaching to help students understand that texts are constructed, convey particular sociocultural values, and invite readers to take up certain positions (which may be resisted).

It is important to note that explicit teaching is not necessarily synonomous with telling. Explicit teaching occurs when a teacher structures a literacy event so that students are consciously focusing on part of the whole, and are developing their ability to talk and think about that part at a metalevel. This focusing could be brought about through teacher questions, strategies like reciprocal teaching (Palincsar & Brown, 1986) or joint construction of a text (Hancock & Leaver, 1994), teacher modeling (Norton, 1992), or direct instruction accompanied by student exercises and drills. But it is crucial to remember Gee's claim (see page 6 of this chapter) that learning does not result in the same kind of fluent performance as acquisition. The implication is that decontextualized teaching and learning evidenced in repetitive drills and exercises is of little or no value if it is isolated from meaningful contexts in which students are required to transfer knowledge and skills, synthesizing the parts back into the whole. That is, the classroom program must give students opportunities to practice the automatic orchestration of the complex elements that constitute reading in contexts that provide for significant outcomes.

Reid (1997) argues for "the engaged production of social texts for real purposes" (p. 150), so that students learn to read and write about things that matter in ways that count inside and outside the classroom. We do not serve our students well if the emphasis on explicit teaching means that the classroom program has no real purposes, audiences, or tasks that students perceive as socially useful and in which something hangs on the outcome (Badger & Wilkinson, 1998). Students will become powerful literacy users only if explicit teaching offers them many opportunities to use information and strategies purposefully in contexts that matter and are meaningful to them. Two things—explicitness by the teacher and purposeful use by the students—need to have a symbiotic relationship. It is relatively straightforward to construct writing and speaking tasks that are holistic and have social relevance. It is less straightforward to construct reading tasks that exemplify the same principles. However, the work of educators like O'Brien (1994, 1995, 1997, 1998) at the elementary level and Janks (1993) and Morgan (1992) at the middle school level suggest pedagogical possibilities for teachers. And, the work of the teachers represented in this volume also shows what can be achieved in teaching reading.

Concerns About Explicit Teaching

Explicit teaching is an essential part of the literacy curriculum, but rigorous teacher decision making is needed so that it is used to promote students' learning in a timely manner and in appropriate circumstances. Otherwise, it can be fraught with problems.

First, undue emphasis on explicit teaching can lead to a fragmented curriculum of drills and trial runs, which students never have a chance to synthesize into meaningful wholes that fulfill worthwhile and significant social functions inside and outside the classroom.

Second, a transmission model of learning can easily become predominant, with students expected to learn what is taught either from very few examples or through rote memorization and repetitive application. Relatively simple information, like the letter *s* usually represents an /s/ sound, may be learned by some students in one or two lessons. But most students will need many experiences with the letter *s*: in the many fonts in which it can be represented, in different letter strings, in different positions within a word, and in different words before they are able to decode it automatically and independently in both upper- and lowercase. For more complex information, like what constitutes a sentence, students need multiple examples over an extended period of time before they come to a fully developed understanding of the term. A transmission view of teaching and learning also can return us very easily to a "blame-the-victim" mentality (I taught it, but they didn't learn it), in which students rather than the curriculum or the pedagogy become the problem.

A third concern is that the curriculum may become reductionist. In the effort to isolate and explicitly teach particular parts of complex wholes, students may be given simplistic definitions and superficial examples. When students are introduced to complex literary concepts like metaphor, irony, and satire, for example, then they will benefit from an initial definition or description. Of necessity, these will be simplistic and reductionist. If students are to develop mature understandings of the complex concepts behind the labels, then they need to read, identify, and discuss multiple examples over time. Even the concept behind the label *sentence* is deceptively difficult, and students will need many examples and constant instruction and discussion over many years of schooling before they can correctly recognize and use sentences in all their variety. By focusing on either parts or just a few examples, explicit teaching can emphasize surface features at the expense of depth and complexity. Given undue emphasis, explicit teaching can also pull teachers back into the competency driven curriculum, in which constant (standardized) testing of isolated knowledge and skills demeans the complexity of literacy learning and teaching and devalues the cyclic, incremental curriculum with its emphasis on relevant, transferrable, and lifelong learning.

A fourth concern is that focusing on explicit teaching may mean that information is emphasized at the expense of metalevel understandings. For example, an investigation of the processes and strategies used by fluent readers may become subordinated to teaching about decoding. Concentration on the linguistic structures and features of a particular genre may lead students to think that there is only one correct form, or a particular cultural form may be valorized over others. This often happens with narrative, in which the European, chronologically linear, orientation-complication-resolution-coda story is presented as the exemplar of narrative form.

A fifth concern is that explicit teaching can make the values and attitudes in the classroom, which teachers hold unconsciously, even more powerful, marginalizing those students from homes and communities that do not share the same values and attitudes. Educators can become so involved in making explicit what they want students to do, know, and learn, and so diligent in deconstructing texts and in promoting particular strategies and ways of operating, that they fail to interrogate the values and beliefs that support what is being promoted.

Asking questions such as the following can help to make the classroom a place where all students' experiences and backgrounds are valued and given importance:

Is what is valued in the classroom congruent with what is valued in the students' homes and communities?

Which students may be marginalized by what is happening here?

How can bridges be built between the literacies valued by students' homes and communities and those valued by the school?

How can students learn to value the different kinds of discourses that are demanded of them, particularly those that count outside the classroom?

The possible problems resulting from these questions must not be used as an excuse for neglecting explicit teaching in the classroom. Research into classroom literacy teaching has shown clearly that teaching does need to be more explicit (Ludwig & Herschell, 1998), and factors that will help teachers to achieve this are beginning to emerge (Anstey, 1998). There is no doubt that explicit teaching is a crucial part of an effective reading curriculum. The significance of explicit teaching lies in its potential to assist all students to learn the discourses that are essential for successful participation in a highly literate society. Unless it is embedded within a classroom pedagogy that also promotes acquisition through the use of holistic reading activities for socially significant purposes, explicit teaching will be limited in what it can help students to achieve.

References

Alloway, N., & Gilbert, P. (1998). Reading literacy test data: Benchmarking success? *Australian Journal of Language and Literacy, 21*(3), 249–261.

Anstey, M. (1998). Being explicit about literacy instruction. *Australian Journal of Language and Literacy, 21*(3), 206–221.

Badger, L., & Wilkinson, L. (1998). Literacy assessment of students from poor and diverse communities: Changing the programs, changing the outcomes. *Australian Journal of Language and Literacy, 21*(2), 147–158.

Badger, L., & Wilkinson, L. (1999). Assessing students' writing: The myth of the level playing field. In B. Doecke (Ed.), *Responding to students' writing: Continuing conversations*. Norwood, SA: Australian Association for the Teaching of English.

Cambourne, B. (1988). *The whole story: Natural learning and the acquisition of literacy in the classroom*. Auckland, NZ: Ashton Scholastic.

Clyne, M. (1996). Writing, testing and culture, Responding to students' writing. *Idiom*, Special No.1, 104–111.

Comber, B., Badger, L., Nixon, H., & Pitt, J. (1997). *Socio-economically disadvantaged students and the acquisition of school literacies: Pilot study*. Executive summary (Vol. 1). Underdale, SA: University of South Australia.

Comber, B., Green, B., Lingard, B., & Luke, A. (1998). Literacy debates and public education: A question of "crisis"? In A. Reid (Ed.), *Going public: Education, policy and public education in Australia*. Belconnen, ACT: Australian Curriculum Studies Association and Centre for the Study of Public Education, University of South Australia.

Connell, R.W. (1992). *Measuring up: Assessment, evaluation and educational disadvantage* (ACSA Teaching Resource, No. 2). Belconnen, ACT: Australian Curriculum Studies Association.

Connell, R.W. (1993). *Schools and social justice*. Toronto, ON: Our Schools/Our Selves Production.

Connell, R.W., Johnston, K.M., & White, V.M. (1994). The issue of poverty and educational measurement. In E. Hatton (Ed.), *Understanding teaching: Curriculum and the social context of schooling*. Sydney, NSW: Harcourt Brace.

Cumming, J.J., Wyatt-Smith, C.M., Ryan, J., & Doig, S.M. (1998). *The literacy-curriculum interface: The literacy demands of the curriculum in post-compulsory schooling*. Executive summary. Brisbane, QLD: Department of Education, Employment, and Youth Affairs and Griffith University.

Delpit, L.D. (1988). The silenced dialogue: Power and pedagogy in educating other people's children. *Harvard Educational Review, 58*, 280–298.

Eveline, J. (1994). The politics of advantage. *Australian Feminist Studies*, Autumn, 129–154.

Freebody, P. (1992). Inventing cultural-capitalist distinctions in the assessment of HSC papers: Coping with inflation in an era of "literacy crisis." In F. Christie (Ed.), *Literacy in social processes* (pp. 96–108). Darwin, NT: Northern Territory Press.

Freebody, P., Ludwig, C., & Gunn, S. (1995). *Everyday literacy practices in and out of school in low socio-economic urban communities*. Executive Summary. Brisbane, QLD: Griffith University.

Freebody, P., & Luke, A. (1990). Literacies' programs: Debates and demands in a cultural context. *Prospect: Journal of Adult Migrant Education Programs, 5*(3), 7–16

Freppon, P.A., & Dahl, K.L. (1998). Balanced instruction: Insights and considerations. *Reading Research Quarterly, 33*, 240–251.

Gee, J. (1990). *Social linguistics and literacy: Ideology in discourses*. Basingstoke, UK: Falmer Press

Goodman, K.S. (1986). *What's whole in whole language?* Portsmouth, NH: Heinemann.

Green, B., Hodgens, J., & Luke, A. (1997). Debating literacy in Australia: History lessons and popular f(r)ictions. *Australian Journal of Language and Literacy, 20*(1), 6–24

Halliday, M.A.K. (1994). *An introduction to functional grammar* (2nd ed.). London: Edward Arnold.

Hancock, J., & Leaver, C. (1994). *Major teaching strategies for English*. Melbourne, VIC: Australian Reading Association.

Holdaway, D. (1979). *The foundations of literacy*. Sydney, NSW: Ashton Scholastic.

Janks, H. (Ed.). (1993). Critical language awareness series (five booklets). Johannesburg, South Africa: Hodder & Stoughton and Witwatersrand University Press.

An Introduction to the Explicit Teaching of Reading

LoBianco, J., & Freebody, P. (1997). *Australian literacies*. Canberra, ACT: Language Australia.

Ludwig, C., & Herschell, P. (1998). The power of pedagogy: Routines, school literacy practices and outcomes. *Australian Journal of Language and Literacy, 21*(1), 67–83.

Morgan, W. (1992). A post-structuralist English classroom: The example of Ned Kelly. Carlton, VIC: Victoria Association for the Teaching of English.

Norton, D.E. (1992). Engaging children in literature: Modeling inferencing of characterization. *The Reading Teacher, 46*, 64–67.

O'Brien, J. (1994). Show Mum you love her: Taking a new look at junk mail. *Reading, 28*(1), 43–46.

O'Brien, J. (1995). Teaching critical reading to young students (Broadsheet 6). In *Texts: The heart of the English Curriculum* (Series 1). Adelaide, SA: Department of Education and Children's Services.

O'Brien, J. (1997). Happy Mother's Day!: Deconstructing Mother's Day catalogues. In *Texts: The heart of the English Curriculum* (Series 2, Broadsheet 5). Adelaide, SA: Department of Education, Training, and Employment.

O'Brien, J. (1998). Experts in Smurfland. In M. Knobel & A. Healy (Eds.), *Critical literacies in the primary classroom* (pp. 13–26). Newtown, NSW: Primary English Teaching Association.

Palincsar, A.S., & Brown, A.L. (1986). Interactive teaching to promote independent learning from text. *The Reading Teacher, 39*, 771–777.

Reid, J. (1997). Generic practice. *Australian Journal of Language and Literacy, 20*(2), 148–155.

Stuckey, J.E. (1991). *The violence of literacy*. Portsmouth, NH: Boynton/Cook.

White, V., & Young, S. (1989). *Disadvantaged Schools Program directory: Sources of information about the program*. North Ryde, NSW: Sociology Department, Macquarie University.

Wilkinson, L. (1995). Explicit teaching. In *Cornerstones* (Module 7, pp. 59–71). Adelaide, SA: Department of Education and Children's Services.

Chapter Two

"It's Just a Different Answer": Exploring Point of View

Judy Smith

Judy Smith was teaching a school entry class of 5-year-olds (called Receptions in South Australia) when she decided to focus her research on teaching point of view. She chose this aspect of her literacy program because it was now an official part of the early literacy curriculum, and she had not been satisfied with the learning outcomes in this area of her teaching for some years.

A successful early-years teacher of many years, Judy has a broad repertoire of teaching strategies that she draws on as she reflects on students' responses and plans her next step. When she began this unit of work, the core strategy she used was to record students' responses in a Big Book format and to revisit them. By reflecting on the children's responses, Judy became aware of the complexities of some of the tasks she gave them and realized the necessity of making explicit through clear rewards the types of answers that she sought.

When I began my research, explicit teaching meant giving clear directions and watching for (and following up on) any misunderstandings. As a teacher I have always reflected on my practice and have focused on areas that needed professional repair. Telling traditional stories from another point of view had always encouraged great discussions and drama presentations, but did the children really believe the wolf in "The Three Little Pigs" was allowed a point of view? I suspect not.

I set out to explore the notion of point of view and to be able to see if I could answer the following question with some success: Do children really understand and know point of view? I set four goals that I wanted my students to know and understand:

1. Understand the meaning of point of view.
2. Show acceptance of different points of view.

3. Express a point of view on a varied range of everyday experiences.
4. Select print media articles and express a point of view orally, visually, and in writing.

If these goals were achieved, my long-term goal was to develop an assessment that could show the students' understanding of point of view, and provide them with the opportunity to seek and discuss their parents' view about the same task.

To keep the project within a workable and visible framework, I decided to base all activities on a Big Book format, which proved to be one of the strengths of the whole exercise. Yet the decision to do it was made for the following reasons:

- **Motivation**: Sharing Big Books results in enjoyment and group stimulus among junior primary children.
- **Practicality**: Keeping all the pieces together when a major move was going to occur during the project was important.
- **Revisits**: The class could regularly review their previous opinions and decisions. Discussing the issues a number of times with parents, teachers, and other students enabled the students to strengthen their own ideas and opinions.

What Did I Do?

I knew how easily some 5-year-olds formulate their point of view to agree with that of the teacher, and I wanted to change this. The title of the Big Book was simply *Point of View*, and the title page posed the question, Can you see another point of view? When I asked the children if they knew what point of view meant, they had no correct answers. So we began our exploration of point of view.

First Week: Nursery Rhymes

I decided to begin with a familiar nursery rhyme, so all the children had the opportunity to respond to a well-known topic. Some wrapping paper with a "Hey-Diddle-Diddle" theme provided the first resource. I stuck two pictures, one of the cat with his fiddle and one of the cow jumping over the moon (see Figure 1), on the page and posed two written questions:

What might the cow be thinking about the cat?
What might the cat be thinking about the cow?

FIGURE 1   The Cat and the Cow

We then brainstormed the children's answers and discussed these two points of view. The children were content to listen to different points of view and happily moved on to a third question:

What would you think if you saw a cow jumping over a moon?

"It's just a dream," said one student, and "When he comes down he'll break his legs," said another.

The students came up with different answers: some accepting that it could not happen and others responding as if it could. These children were used to offering different interpretations for a fanciful picture. My next step was to move to the real world.

Second Week: Play Equipment

The play equipment was about to be roped off for a week, providing an opportunity for our next point-of-view exploration. Anna was sent outside with a parent helper to do two drawings showing the same playground equipment from different positions. Photographs to support her sketches were also taken. The two drawings were then shared on the Big Book pages. I wanted to explore the notion of a right answer, as I suspected this was possibly a more important notion to 5-year-olds than that of having a different point of view. I asked the children to look at both of Anna's sketches (see Figure 2 on page 16) and to discuss their answers to my question:

FIGURE 2   Anna's Sketches

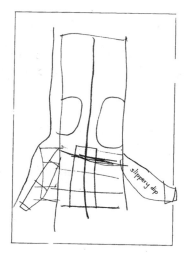

Do these two drawings show the same playground equipment?

A vote was taken and 16 children replied "no" and 2 replied "yes." Outside we discovered the correct answer, and during this conversation Matthew said "Oh yes. It (the equipment) can be seen in different ways." This was one 5-year-old's explanation of point of view. I noted that no other child showed this insight. At this point I realized the complexities of point of view for children of this age.

It was clear that we had just begun the complex task of exploring point of view, because the students clearly showed that having the correct answer was more important than accepting differing points of view. The fact that this second activity resulted from a student's observations and recordings satisfied my strong belief that experiences relating to student interests were powerful motivators for learning. Further spontaneous observations about how the equipment looked from different positions were noted during lunch break.

The next day, two students looking at the new veranda near their classroom had this conversation:

"What does it look like from where you're standing?" asked one student. He then gave a description.

The second student replied, "It's different here. It looks like one pole going along, not lots of poles like you said."

These playground conversations indicated that my students were beginning to recognize and view their visual world in a critical way. I was excited about these observations. Our discussions were already influencing what the children noticed and found worth sharing.

Third Week: Newspaper Photos

In this activity, I intervened with a resource, which I chose to do because of my keenness to link point of view with media photos from the daily paper. My long-term aim was to develop an assessment in this area. Finding a picture that was motivational for a 5-year-old was a challenge. After much page turning, the local weekly paper provided one—a front-cover enlargement of a man just taking his next step, having stepped in dog waste in the local park. I posed the following written questions:

What would the man think?
What would the dog think?
What do you think?

I anticipated that this picture would create a conversation among the children, and it was interesting to note the different biases in the point-of-view answers:

"Yuk," and "I'll have to wipe my feet before I go inside" were common responses to the first and third questions. The dog on the other hand had more daring answers:

"Oh yes, that's what I wanted to happen."

"Ha, ha. That man's going to make a mess on his floor."

I felt I had made a good choice because this picture has proven to be popular when we revisit and discuss our point-of-view book. Many conversations about point of view take place when this page is presented; motivation as a teaching strategy was obvious here.

I had anticipated that this project would conclude after four to five sessions, but the students asked, "What are we going to do next?" This student-initiated request for a learning focus stimulated me to look for the next media resource. I had asked the students to look for appropriate pictures for discussing point of view, but none were placed in the plastic pocket clipped to the Big Book stand. They all were confident now in offering suggestions and discussing their ideas with one another.

Fourth Week: Man in Danger?

I now looked for another media picture that would challenge their thinking. Again, the local newspaper provided just the picture: a man being jolted by static electricity. I asked the following question:

Is this man in danger?

I asked the children to vote "yes" or "no" because I felt that they were now confident and comfortable with presenting a verbal point of view. However, they remained easily influenced by what appeared to be happening and were not prepared to support their view if other views differed from their own. I anticipated most would vote "yes." Eighteen did; three voted "no." This time the students wrote their answers and shared them with a partner and the whole group. Examples were pasted in the Big Book.
Common "yes" answers:

He's in danger because his hair is on fire.

He's in danger because he's getting his neck strangled.

He's in danger because fireworks are coming over him.

The three "no" answers:

He's not in danger because he is strangling himself.

He's not in danger. He looks like he is going to fall down.

He's not in danger. He is just a bit scared.

When it was revealed that the picture was of a man doing an experiment at a science and technology centre, there were a few groans from some of the "yes" students. Belief that their own point of view was still valued needed to be affirmed. At this point two significant things happened. After we had discovered the correct answer, I again instigated discussion about whether it was OK that people had different points of view about the picture. "Yes," said Jonathan, "it just means they have different answers."

The group appeared satisfied by this answer, and I turned back to the title page and wrote Jonathan's definition under the words *point of view*. I was beginning to feel more successful in teaching point of view, but I realized it would need far more explanation and planned experiences before the students had any depth of understanding.

I could see that we still had a lot more work to do before there was a class understanding that a variety of views are acceptable and valued.

Fifth Week: Morning Glory and Wilfred Gordon

Within a current unit on flowers, we had made a divided collection box and added different varieties of flowers daily. The morning glory vine provided the motivation for our next discovery about point of view. I anticipated the students would be able to draw the morning glory from different positions or perspectives (see Figure 3), similar to the

FIGURE 3   Morning Glory

Morning Glory

drawings Anna had done in the play-equipment activity (see Figure 2 on page 16) and had put in the Big Book.

During this exercise children's comments were beginning to show that learning was taking place. "Oh, yours is just drawn from a different side to mine, but it's still the same isn't it?" and "I looked down on mine and you looked at its side" were noted examples. Some children asked to have their drawings put in the Big Book to show how their drawings were different. Point-of-view discussions were occurring spontaneously, and I was beginning to feel that exploring point of view through the stimulus of a shared Big Book was proving to be a well-chosen strategy for 5-year-olds.

Having to make a temporary move to the library one afternoon provided a surprise resource for this study. A picture book taken from the classroom shelf to use as "quiet time together before we plan what we do" was Mem Fox's *Wilfred Gordon Mc-Donald Partridge*. What a discussion we had about Mrs. Jordan believing memory was something warm, Miss Mitchell knowing that it made you laugh, and Miss Cooper having lost hers. Comments showed that the students found the characters' impressions acceptable: "They were all right about what a memory is; they just had different ideas about it," said one student. They chose to illustrate some of their own sad and happy memories and selected memory pictures were added to the Big Book.

At this stage I felt point of view was becoming a discovery that Lyn Wilkinson (personal conversation, January 14, 1997) said was "leaving nothing merely implied," and that it was "not just teaching kids the obvious." I was beginning to feel a strong ownership of the project and was keen to see where the students would take us in the following weeks.

Sixth Week: House for Sale

At this point I introduced another picture from the daily paper. (I still had not received any pictures from the students.) The picture was of a house for sale, and I asked the question:

Do you like this house? Yes or no?

I anticipated there would be a higher number of "yes" votes because the house was a big bungalow like many of their own houses, and they would reject a right or wrong answer and accept different points of view. There were 18 "yes" votes and 3 "no" votes. Why did the "yes" voters like the house? One of these voters said, "It was big, it had a nice garden, looked friendly, and had grass to play on." No voters said, "It's not a stair house" and "There's no leaves on the tree." My anticipated outcomes for the students proved to be correct, and as I reflected on my goals, I felt positive about the way the students were accepting and expecting different points of view. At this point, the children's interest was driving our explorations. Many were asking what was in the Big Book for the day.

Seventh Week: Peter, a Bee, and a Flower

To further increase discussions, I focused next on our flower unit of work. I also wanted to develop a partner activity so that all children had a chance to share a view and develop their ability to support it. I hastily created the television cartoon character Bart Simpson's cousin Peter and sketched him with a flowering plant and a bee (see Figure 4).

I then posed the following questions:

> What is the bee's point of view?
> What is the flower's point of view?
> What is happening in this picture?
> What is Peter's point of view about what is happening in this picture?

I purposely did not allow whole-class discussion as I wanted to see the results of the partner discussion. The students surprised me with the diversity of their answers:

> The bee was mad because Peter cut the flower. He stinged Peter and he died.
> Peter is going to cut the flower, and he's going to throw it in the bin.

FIGURE 4   Peter, A Bee, and A Flower

The bee is going to sting the man because he wanted the pollen.
The flower thinks it's not OK because it is cross with the bee buzzing
around it and the man because he is going to cut the petals off.

I was feeling comfortable with the development of the task; however, I had not
had any success in getting newspaper pictures from the students, so I offered a reward
to the first person who brought a newspaper picture for our point-of-view book. Two
students responded the next day and four responded by the end of the week. I continued to encourage the students to bring pictures, because my aim was to encourage
them to use the print media, in particular, Adelaide's only newspaper and the free local newspaper. I regarded the students bringing their own pictures as an important
step toward looking critically at print media in their family life. The transfer between
home and school needed to be strengthened. So the challenge continued for another
week, and we were ready for the next page.

Eighth Week: Lunch-time Dilemma

A problem at lunch had arisen for a group of girls, who always bought frozen
fruit drinks, which took all of the lunch hour to eat and inhibited any time for play.
This provided me with a way to problem solve using point of view, so I set up a role-
play task:

Is it a good idea to have a frozen drink at lunch time? Yes or no?

I was confident that my point of view would be addressed: that buying frozen
drinks at lunch was not a good idea because it prevented students from having any play.
Wrong. In fact, it was not mentioned. Four groups of four students chose to support
that it was a good idea, and one group chose the opposite. One group worked on a
role play showing that if a student had one dollar to spend and bought a frozen drink,
it was good because there would still be 60 cents left to spend. The group that thought
it was not a good idea structured their role play showing that if you took an unfin-
ished frozen drink to class after lunch you would be in trouble. The lesson showed me
the difference between student and teacher views on a class problem. I was surprised
by these responses, but pleased that the children were not looking to me for answers.

Ninth Week: Sprouting Potato

One morning, Amanda came to school with a shriveled and sprouting potato.
Little did I know I was about to receive another sharp rise in my learning curve. She
announced, "Mum said can we guess what this is." It posed no problem for me, but

FIGURE 5 Sprouting Potatoes

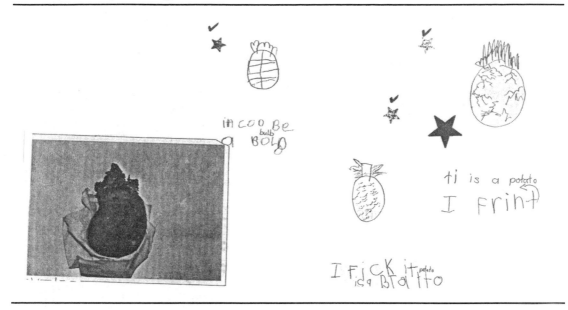

when I asked the children, "What do you think it is from your point of view?" no one had a response.

I decided this was the time to introduce individual written responses. I asked the students to sketch the object (see Figure 5) and then answer the question. With my throw-away comment, "You might write that in your point of view it might be a black cat," the task began. The sketches were completed quickly and showed the main details of the shriveled spud. The written answers would reveal how carefully teachers of young children need to be not to influence the students' points of view toward their own.

The student responses revealed open self-expression. Six students had answers that indicated a clear understanding of the meaning of point of view in this task. Each had formulated a point of view that was not influenced by my initial comment:

> It could be a bulb.
> I think it is a potato.
> A potato.
> It is a potato.
> I think it's a flower.
> It's a pumpkin.

Each of the six responses demonstrated that forming a point of view involves thinking, formulating, and supporting one's own opinion without being influenced by

FIGURE 6 Two Student Responses

a sunburst

SdOBSI

a Bdak cat

---

others. None of the six students wanted to change their point of view even though it differed with the majority of their peers. Each was prepared to express his or her ideas in written form and present them during group sharing time.

Among the rest the tally was nine black cats, one black turtle, and two frozen drinks. Two examples (see Figure 6) of the work by students who were still prepared to accept the teacher's throw-away comment without question are as follows:

> It's a frozen drink.
> A black cat.

This was a powerful argument for explicit teaching. I needed a clear strategy to affirm responses when students expressed what they believed, and valued their own viewpoint enough to support it against an adult point of view.

The work of the six students who indicated ownership of their points of view were glued onto the next page of the Big Book. I gave each an individual star sticker and a large red star sticker for their combined efforts, which were powerful, positive, and explicit awards in my class. The impact was significant. Gasps of "Wow" greeted the first viewing of the starred responses. These rewards made it clear to some of the students that valuing and standing up for one's own response was important. On one of the pages I also wrote

> Everyone else said nine black cats, one black turtle, and two frozen drinks.

Were these people thinking about their own point of view?

We discussed these suggestions and reasoned why these students had presented these ideas, but most importantly we laughed at why the vast majority of students had allowed someone else's point of view to influence their own. This page became a very powerful teaching and learning page. Whenever we revisited the Big Book, this page was chosen often for further discussion. This was a powerful insight for me. I was struck with how important it is to continually monitor students' responses—to take nothing for granted.

Tenth Week: The Blind Men and the Elephant

The move back to our freshly painted class was affecting our present environment. Our classroom resources were being packed again, so I introduced a traditional East Indian story, "The Blind Men and the Elephant," which graphically illustrates different points of view. In this story, six blind men touch a different part of an elephant, which gives each a very different idea of what an elephant must look like, and an argument results about which point of view is correct.

The students accepted the blind men's different points of view and that none were right or wrong. This activity did not produce the same enthusiastic response as the class-related activities, so I returned to the texts chosen by the children.

Eleventh Week: The Jockey

By now there were several newspaper photographs in the point of view pocket, and the children were asking when we were going to talk about them. I introduced Ben's picture of a jockey and a horse showing the jockey falling under the horse's neck, which some of the class had already commented on.

The students were asked to choose and write two different points of view from the following questions:

> What is the horse's point of view about what is happening in this picture?
> What is the jockey's point of view about what is happening in this picture?
> What is your point of view about what is happening in the picture?

Although I had anticipated that the students would write simple answers, I was surprised by the range of ideas and how confidently they spoke about, accepted, and compared their ideas. All the students had clear, defensible points of view, which showed they could distinguish among different views of one situation:

Horse's:	Goodie!
Jockey's:	Oh no!
Me:	I think they should stop the race.
Jockey's :	I'm scared.
Horse's:	Oh no. That jockey he fell off again.
Horse's point of view:	The man is falling off me.
Jockey's point of view:	I better hold on next time.

I was feeling comfortable and pleased about the goals I had set and that my teaching was explicit in making clear to students when they were overly influenced by others and when they were able to explain their own opinions. I chose one more activity before leaving our exploration of point of view.

Last Activity: Houses for Sale

When we moved back to our classroom, we had few available resources. So as an activity, I asked the students to express points of view about *luxury*. I showed them a group of houses for sale from the local newspaper (Figure 7) and used a media heading as the reading focus.

I thought the meaning of *luxury* could prove difficult for my 5-year-olds, but I had introduced the term to them in week six and asked them the questions:

If you could live in luxury, which house would you choose and why?
What is your point of view?

The diversity of the answers clearly indicated the confidence every student felt in expressing point of view and accepting those of others. Statements like, "Yes, I wouldn't have thought of that" and "That's a good idea" were genuine. Four of the written responses were as follows:

I would choose number eight because it has got upstairs and a garden.
I would choose number six because it looks nice and has a fire place.
I love fires.
I would choose number five because I like the garden.
I would choose number four because it has a big tree for climbing.

The children continued to talk about and defend their choices as they left for lunch. I felt satisfied that they were all well on the way to being able to form, express, and justify points of view in a variety of situations. I was not sure, however, if some still may be easily swayed by an influential adult.

FIGURE 7   Point of View About Luxury

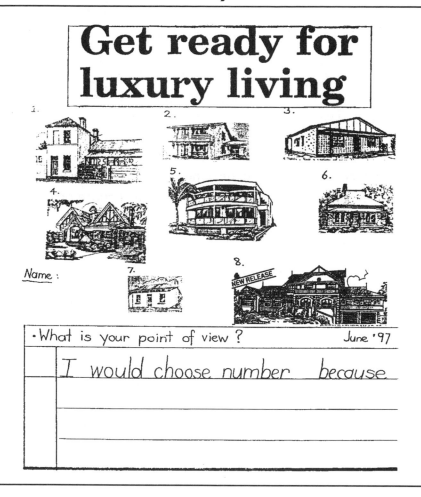

Final Reflections

As I reflected on the point-of-view activities we had shared through our Big Book, I felt satisfied with the explicit teaching that had occurred. Students had been asked to respond to a variety of tasks, which enabled them to distinguish between fact and fantasy, fact and opinion, why people see things differently, how to understand different points of view, and why we need to justify our points of view.

The Big Book activities had challenged the children to explore and understand that point of view is about interpreting, choosing, or imagining in response to a variety of texts, and being able to justify a response. An imaginative response for a fictional situation was needed for "What might the cow be thinking?" while recognition that two pictures could be of the same object was the focus for the play-equipment and the morning glory activities. "Is this man in danger?" asked for an interpretation with a reason for a trick photo. An opinion and a justification were involved in "Is it a good idea to have a frozen drink at lunch time?" and "What could the jockey be thinking?" Teaching point of view is not about teaching kids the obvious. It is about students listening carefully to the task, forming an opinion, and being able to justify that opinion.

Our exploration had gone way beyond seeking responses to traditional stories such as "The Three Little Pigs." It had offered a variety of texts, with discussion questions asking for different types of responses such as giving a preference with reasons, an opinion with justifications, or a fanciful response. The students had gained confidence in expressing points of view orally and in writing, and in understanding and accepting other points of view. The Big Book had become a valuable resource for us to revisit and add to when the opportunity was presented. It also remained an explicit reminder of what can happen when we are influenced by others.

Children's Literature Reference

Fox, M. (1984). *Wilfred Gordon McDonald Partridge*. Adelaide, SA: Omnibus.

Chapter Three

Not Just Onions! Exploring Layers of Meaning in Texts

Lynda Matthews

As well as being a Years 1 and 2 classroom teacher, Lynda Matthews is a literacy coordinator in a large rural school. Each year all the Year 3 and Year 5 students in South Australia take standardized basic skills tests. As literacy coordinator, Lynda analyzed the data from the language test for information that could be used to improve teaching and learning in the school. The questions that posed the most consistent difficulty for children involved one of four roles of the literate person—that of text analyst (Freebody & Luke, 1990). [These four roles had been introduced in the *Cornerstones* early literacy inservice program (see Preface, p. vi).] The children needed to understand that texts present points of view (see Chapter 2) and that authors and illustrators carefully plan to present these views, often by conveying a number of messages at the same time. These messages are not always immediately obvious.

In her research project, Lynda decided to make explicit the ways texts operate at a number of levels. She explored with her students several carefully constructed texts, which would lead them to discover the different levels of meaning. She used think-aloud to reveal her own construction of meanings: she talked about the cues she was using, the tentative predictions she was working on, and the conclusions she was drawing, and she invited the students to contribute to her meaning making. She also provided a metalanguage: *text*, *top story*, and *bottom story*.

Having decided that across the school the students needed more skills in text analysis, I needed to develop a strategy in this area. My class was the obvious place to start and I began by asking what texts were. I wanted students to be able to use the term *texts* to cover a wide range of language forms. They worked in groups of four with a leader, a recorder, an observer, and a timer to discuss the question. The term *texts* had been used to look at different forms of writing, so they had some insight into what was required. When the groups came back together, I summarized their answers on the board:

Texts

words	books	writing
radio	talking	listening
reading and sharing ideas	TV	
it's how people make us think		

This showed me that the students knew a lot about text. They were ready to go on and look at layers of meaning within text and tell how texts influence them.

Information Gained From Titles

Discussion of the information in titles seemed a natural starting point. We already had looked at the impact of covers and found that authors must choose the title carefully because it creates reader interest.

Without reading the book or showing the cover, I presented Bob Graham's *Rose Meets Mr. Wintergarten* and asked the class what the author wanted them to know about the characters and the story when he chose this title. I wrote the names of the two characters on the board, and the children brainstormed ideas suggested by the title, which might inform them about the characters and the story:

Rose
girl, petals, flower
garden, nice, kind, pretty
rosy cheeks, friendly
smells nice, good, happy
great, lots of friends
brave, colorful, bright

Mr. Wintergarten
man, garden, cold, grey
it's got winter in it
likes winter
cold in it–inside him?
got roots, may be kind
cross, grumpy, lonely

Their task was to draw each character on one piece of paper to show what they already knew about each person (see Figure).

The drawings were outstanding and showed the differences between the characters, which the class had discussed. Post-picture discussion reached the consensus that the story was about how the two characters got together. Their reasoning was "a rose grows in a garden." When I read the story aloud, the students were amazed at how much information the title had given them.

I saw that the children already read a lot into titles.
They had a rich literary background that enabled them to
build complex images from words.

Discovering the Layers

In our next session, I introduced author Margaret Wild whose work is not only emotive and varied, but each of her stories has a story within a story, a meaning beneath the surface story, which I wanted the children to be able to identify. I explained to them that writers sometimes give us more than one story—one that is recognized easily (top story) and another that we are meant to think about (bottom story).

I read to them *My Dearest Dinosaur*, because they had just finished an integrated unit on dinosaurs, and I felt they would have an understanding of the issues involved. My question was What are the different stories in *My Dearest Dinosaur*?

The children knew the story was about a mother dinosaur writing to the father dinosaur, and decided that he was probably dead, which they also recognized as the extinction of the dinosaurs. They easily recognized and elaborated on the levels of meaning within the story and linked the book to the video *Land Before Time* (1988), which they had viewed in the dinosaur unit. Both texts were about the end of the dinosaur age and animals trying to find a place to live and becoming extinct. Both texts involved families of animals who had lost a family member; but one was more about the thoughts and feelings of young dinosaurs, and the other was more about those of older dinosaurs. When they shared this book with their *Big Buddies*, a Year 5 and 6 class with whom they worked, the Buddies were surprised about what the students had discovered and added only that the story could also be about the way people care for each other, even when they are not together. The two groups worked in pairs to make posters about the many meanings in the story.

Although my 5- to 7-year-olds brought much to the texts, the older students added a further dimension, which they shared in groups openly and sensitively with their younger Buddies.

The next Margaret Wild book, *Toby*, about a family dog that had died, showed the different ways in which family members reacted to Toby growing old. It showed how different people experience and cope with the same event. The children talked in class and with their parents at home about their own experiences with death. I used other Margaret Wild books to explore different issues and different levels of stories. We discussed top story and bottom story or the story underneath. The children recognized and became excited about discovering levels of meaning and sharing them with others:

> "I never thought of that!"
> "Oh yeah, that's another story."
> "That story is really sad; the top story isn't so bad."

Books for Discovering Layers

Title	Topic
Sam's Sunday Dad	Divorce and different family structures
A Bit of Company	Siblings, new arrivals, finding friendship in unexpected places
Remember Me	Alzheimer's disease, memories
Creatures in the Beard	Attitudes toward animals
All the Better to See You With	Glasses, family roles
Space Travellers	Homelessness, imagination
Big Cat Dreaming	Relationships with grandparents
The Very Best of Friends	Friendship and death
Let the Celebrations Begin	Hardship, joy, survival
Mr. Nick's Knitting	Friendship, absent friends
Going Home	Hospitalization, fantasy
Toby	Death, relationships, coping

The books that worked particularly well included issues that linked to the current experiences and concerns of children in the class; for example, meeting new friends, getting new glasses, and dealing with a grandmother's death. The children had opportunities to express these concerns during quiet time or in class meetings.

One of the books that worked well for modeling the process of uncovering layers of meaning in a whole-class situation was *All the Better to See You With*. After reading the book together, we explored it in stages for the ways in which Margaret Wild created her story. I asked questions that were clear and that enabled students to look critically at the story and pictures. I began with the cover and title and moved through the book page by page asking myself questions and thinking aloud as I modeled my reasoning. I asked the students to help with the answers at each stage, talking through the steps, discovering the links that were made, and supporting our answers with the information we found. I used the following questions with this book:

> What does the title tell us?
> What do you think the pictures help us to see?
> Tell me about the family—how do you know?
> Tell me about Kate—what gives you that information?
> What do the illustrations tell us about Kate's vision?
> Why doesn't the family know Kate can't see?
> What happened to Kate that made her family realize that Kate can't see?
> What did Kate need?
> How does Kate feel about her glasses?
> How does Margaret Wild let us know she feels that way?
> How does her family feel now?
> Does this story have another story in it—apart from the one about the little girl who needs glasses?
> What is this story and how do you know about it?

I focused on and used three clarifying questions with all the books:

1. How did you know that?
2. What made you think that?
3. How did the author tell you that?

We frequently pondered the three clarifying questions, which helped the students to analyze the way authors' choice of words directs our thinking. At this point I used a strategy from *First Steps* (1993) to highlight how adjectives alter meaning, and how particular words convey images and feelings. The students were asked to write down three words that described the earth and, using these in a group, they were to create an earth chant that began and ended with *earth*. When the groups put them together, the result looked like this:

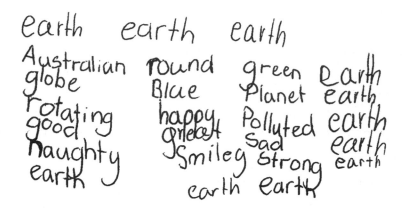

I then asked each group to write two sentences, presenting two different points of view. One group came up with a pair of sentences, which are typical of the sentences devised by the different groups:

We live on a polluted, rotating, sad earth.

We live on a round, green, smiley earth.

 This exercise worked well. The children commented with surprise on the difference one word can make. Over time, working in groups, in pairs, and alone, the children became so good at analyzing stories that I wondered if they would ever simply experience a story.

Analyzing the Media

I realized that the media greatly affects the lives of students. Therefore, I decided we should look at the ways in which the media conveys different messages and how those messages link to what the children already knew about texts. Step one was easy. For homework I asked them to watch a television commercial and then to discuss, write about, and draw pictures using the following questions:

What is the commercial about?
What do the people who made the commercial want us to do?

How do the people who make the commercial make you want to do what they want you to do?

I had the students look at the commercials in the same way they had looked at stories. They discussed the words, pictures, characters, and music. Although music was not an element that had been explored previously, they quickly became aware of the effects of music in the commercials. They had very clear ideas about how the commercials were meant to affect them.

In groups they explored writing their own commercials. They turned to the three original questions for support. Because their commercials would be assessed, students negotiated the criteria for successful completion of the task, deciding to

- make things that they would like to advertise,
- write and enact scripts that would make the rest of the class want to use their product,
- film the commercials, and
- evaluate all the commercials using the following as a measure of success (their idea):
  1. Each child would have $20 to spend.
  2. No product could cost more than $10.
  3. The most successful products would be judged on the number bought and the most money made.
  4. Reasons had to be given for purchases.

The children produced a variety of things, some predictable but some very original: a truck carrying cattle, a wide range of dolls, a drive-yourself car that did everything, a magic butterfly, different foodstuffs, a cubby house, and a pencil that wrote but could not be seen. Because many were beginning writers, they had some difficulty with script writing, but no problems with the dramatics. Some students used music, some used the smaller children to make their products look bigger, and some spent time on sets. Of course, they all had long lists of reasons why everyone should buy their product.

The children easily recognized what the others were trying to achieve. They offered criticism of scenes—not about how good or bad they were, but about the intended purpose; the use and overuse of certain characters; the value of money, and the usefulness of the product. "I didn't really need it!" was a frequent criticism. They appreciated the ways in which other groups had tried to manipulate them: "I liked the way they made the truck so big and then had Harry (the smallest boy in the class) drive it. William (the tallest boy in class) would have made it look smaller," said one student.

All of us—the parents, the children, and I—were excited by the children's knowledge of possibilities, their awareness of the ways texts manipulate, and their enthusiasm to use this new awareness to influence others. Michael conveyed his conviction about the power of words in this statement to a friend he tried to persuade: "Well, I can change the words to make you do it anyway."

What Was Working

On reflection, I found that two sets of strategies used in the classroom supported and enhanced this unit: motivational and explicit teaching.

Motivational strategies
- Ensure a high level of access to materials and information by allowing students to use or to suggest for class any books or other materials in the classroom, library, or home.
- Build high self-esteem in students by expecting them to be successful.
- Maintain high levels of motivation within the class community by encouraging positive attitudes toward and ownership of all that happens within the classroom and to the members of the group. Encourage them to take initiative and support one another and the class as a whole.
- Involve parents by developing a class newsletter to alert them to what is happening in their child's classroom. Also encourage parents to (1) interact with their children about classroom events, (2) have family discussions about homework, (3) discuss books with their children rather than simply listen to them read, (4) follow up on class-initiated ideas and make links with the home discourse, and (5) invite their children to relate what they do at school to what they do at home.

Explicit teaching strategies
- Set clear, positive guidelines for classroom behaviors that are to be student owned and maintained.
- Develop clear, collaborative learning processes during the students' time in class.
- Negotiate assessment so that students know what they are aiming for.
- Think aloud in class with students, explaining what is being done and why.
- Reflect aloud, which allows students to know what has worked or has not worked well and to consider new options. My decision making is exposed, made explicit, to the children.
- Make explicit to students class issues and topics, contexts, and purposes so they are able to be explicit to their parents about classroom events.

- Involve students in setting goals, providing resources, and establishing timetables. Suggesting direction, activities, and structure enables them to own all that happens in the classroom.

My Reflections

This was one of the most interesting and exciting units of work done by this class. Children and parents were very involved and became aware of the importance of the subtle messages received by text recipients from print and other media. I observed the following benefits and positive results from this unit:

- Using the same books with the young children and older children provided both classes with different and enhanced perspectives and reinforced positive attitudes in the young children. Their knowledge gave them power.
- Having the children explain their goals and thoughts to their parents clarified issues for children and increased the involvement of parents and their understanding of the complexity of literacy issues. The parents could relate things that happen at home to what their children were doing at school.
- The children noticed advertising in the streets and shops around them and transferred their understanding to this area. I saw and heard children explaining the purpose of advertising rather than just wanting the product.
- Students became more careful about word usage. Adjectives were selected carefully and requests for suggestions were brought up in group editing.
- The students examined books more carefully—particularly the title—before selecting. They recognized titles as indicators of the author's purpose.

The students now understand that people can see the same thing in different ways. I thought I would next launch into critical literacy, but soon found that the children already understood the concept!

References

Cornerstones: Training and development program. (1996). Adelaide, SA: Department of Education and Children's Services.

Freebody, P., & Luke, A. (1990). Literacies' programs: Debates and demands in a cultural context. *Prospect: Journal of Adult Migrant Education Programs, 5*(3), 7–16.

Education Department of Western Australia. (1994). *First steps writing resource book.* Melbourne, VIC: Longman.

Spielberg, S. (Director). (1988). *Land before time*. [Video].

Children's Literature References

Graham, B. (1992). *Rose meets Mr. Wintergarten*. Ringwood, VIC: Viking.

Wild, M. (1991). *A bit of company*. Sydney, NSW: Ashton Scholastic.

Wild, M. (1992). *All the better to see you with*. North Sydney, NSW: Allen and Unwin.

Wild, M. (1996). *Big cat dreaming*. Ringwood, VIC: Viking.

Wild, M. (1986). *Creatures in the beard*. Adelaide, SA: Omnibus.

Wild, M. (1986). *Going home*. Sydney, NSW: Ashton Scholastic.

Wild, M. (1991). *Let the celebrations begin*. Norwood, SA: Omnibus.

Wild, M. (1992). *Mr. Nick's knitting*. Sydney, NSW: Hodder and Stoughton.

Wild, M. (1990). *Remember me*. Sydney, NSW: Margaret Hamilton.

Wild, M. (1992). *Sam's Sunday dad*. Sydney, NSW: Hodder and Stoughton.

Wild, M. (1992). *Space travellers*. Sydney, NSW: Ashton Scholastic.

Wild, M. (1993). *Toby*. Norwood, SA: Omnibus.

Chapter Four

Building on Cultural Capital: Linking Home and School Literacies With Popular Texts

Lyn Shepherd

Lyn Shepherd teaches a Years 2 and 3 class in a primary school where 75 % of the families receive government support because of low income. Twenty-five percent of the students are from non–English speaking backgrounds, 15 % are Aboriginal, and 50 % have been identified as having severe learning difficulties.

The recent amalgamation of the junior and senior schools provided an opportunity for teachers to discover how to better meet the needs of the students and the community and to improve learning. Visiting speakers with expertise in literacy education and equity helped teachers look at ways to

(1) establish a register of the cultural resources within the community,

(2) use popular culture as a literacy and learning tool, and

(3) develop a responsive and flexible literacy curriculum that adapts to the needs of the community.

Out of this work, Lyn decided to teach a unit of learning that linked home and school reading using popular texts. To make clear to parents and students that home texts were valued at schools, she supported the students in creating a magazine by making explicit the different components.

I wanted to build on the students' curriculum by making the links between home and school obvious and by being explicit about the features of popular texts. I was committed to giving students choice, developing their cooperation and independence, ensuring as much as possible that they would experience success, and making their school experiences enjoyable.

I began by learning about the knowledge and experiences that students brought from home. At the same time, the students would become aware of the kinds of reading that were part of their everyday life. I wanted them to see reading as an important and useful part of their home life.

Finding Out What They Read

I surveyed my students using two questions:

What do you read at school?
What do you read at home?

I was confident that I had provided a diverse range of reading material within my classroom, which matched what the students were reading at home. But I was in for a surprise. The students identified 31 types of literature that they read at school (see Figure 1, which also shows the number of students who identified each type).

By far the most popular texts read at school were books, while different texts were read at home (see Figure 2 on page 41). Among the texts read at home, the most popular were magazines, comics, and recipe books. Only four students mentioned books. I had assumed incorrectly that the range of literature in students' homes would be very limited. However, I realized that the most popular forms of reading at home

Figure 1   What Students Read at School

books	20	magazines	3
posters	15	stories	1
words	5	newspapers	6
signs	12	journals	1
boxes	3	writing	5
names	10	jars	5
computer	5	recipes	2
numbers	3	watches	1
blackboard	3	lips	1
bags	2	rhymes	2
charts	10	dictionaries	2
poetry	2	traffic signs	3
procedures	2	notes	3
homework	1	jokes	1
maths	3	music	2
cards	3		

were those least valued at school. Thus the focus for my teaching became how to value home literacies in the school setting.

Figure 2 What Students Read at Home

magazines	15	comics	12
recipe books	9	Goosebumps	8
games	7	books	4
posters	5	charts	4
words	1	lists	1
television guide	3	cereal boxes	5
cards	1	signs	1
alphabet posters	1	computer games	1
puzzles	1	football paper	3
dictionaries	1	jars	1
computer	6		

A Focus on Magazines

For the next term, I focused on magazines because they were the texts most read at home.

To begin, I asked the students to bring magazines from home to share in small groups. I asked them to look through and to identify the elements that made up a magazine, which we listed (see Figure 3).

The students decided to publish their own magazine, *Teddy Magazine*, because we had just completed a unit called the Teddy Bears' Picnic based on the framework of Contextualized Learning[1]. Together we planned, created, and carried out a menu, and recipes. We did the shopping, cooking, and assembled the picnic sets. We sent invitations, arranged the program, and set up a display. The students planned what they

Figure 3 Elements of Magazines

news items	photos	phone numbers
crosswords	contents page	cartoons
addresses	games	gossip columns
tongue twisters	true or false	pictures
jokes	poems	find-a-word
recipes	articles	problems
stories	puzzles	

wanted to do, and I supported them in achieving their goals. The end celebration, which directly reflected those goals, was a Teddy Bears' picnic.

To begin *Teddy Magazine*, we reviewed magazine elements and planned the cover. We wrote a letter to the school services officer and asked her to design the cover. The students formed groups to begin their writing for the magazine. Because we had identified, documented, and reviewed the magazine elements, I assumed the students would understand the layouts of magazines, so I was amazed at what they produced. Advertisements took up whole pages, as did all the components that had been brainstormed: recipes, news items, gossip columns, and crossword puzzles. It did not look at all like a magazine. I had assumed prior knowledge, and now I could see "interactive trouble" (Freebody, Ludwig, & Gunn, 1995) (see Preface, p. vii), which is the miscommunication that occurs between teachers and students.

I thought that by comparing magazines with books, the students would come to realize the difference in structure and components.

Comparing Books With Magazines

We revisited the magazines and focused on layout, and I asked what makes a magazine different from a book and collated the answers:

- Books are about one thing.
- Magazines have more writing.
- Magazines have crosswords, advertisements, games, and more pictures.
- Books have a story and magazines are more like comic books.
- Books have more pages.
- Magazines have lots of photos.
- Books have more writing and magazines have more pictures.

Their responses were quite comprehensive and revealed a clearer understanding of what constitutes a magazine. Obviously my teaching had been more explicit. I was eager for the students to begin writing for the magazine, but they could not put down commercial magazines. They kept reading them, and I was becoming a bit frustrated. Then I realized that the students were enjoying the opportunity of having home literacies valued in the school setting—and they were reading! So I let them continue, realizing that at reading time I had always focused their attention on books—not magazines.

Wanting them to explore the differences between reading books and magazines, I set up discussions and surveys that would allow the students to reflect on themselves as readers and the processes they use to get meaning from the different types of texts. I asked them to write whether they preferred books or magazines and why. Interestingly, 11 students selected books, 8 preferred magazines, and 5 selected both. Their reasons were varied:

Why Students Preferred Books

- Books are easier to read because they don't have so many pictures.
- Books are better.
- Books don't have crosswords.
- Because I like reading.
- Books have easy words and less pages.

Why Students Preferred Magazines

- Because they have more writing.
- Magazines have more pictures.
- I like reading magazines—they have writing and pictures.
- I like reading magazines because I can fill in the words.

Why Students Chose Both

- Because they are good to read.
- It's easy to read them both.

When I asked if a magazine is harder to read, 63 % said "yes." Some of the students gave reasons:

- It has more pages.
- It has more writing.
- It has hard words.
- It has long writing.
- It has lots of different things on one page.
- Because it is long.

Although students preferred to read magazines at home, they also identified magazine reading as more difficult. I reflected on whether students would willingly pick up an adult book. My feeling was that probably they would not, although they are quite comfortable increasing their understanding of the world in which they live through adult magazines—an acknowledged difficult but popular text. Through exploring the students' "cultural capital" (Carrington & Luke, 1997), I gained further insight into the ways in which students were developing their world views. Because they had identified magazines as being difficult to read, I wanted to know who assisted them in reading magazines at home. I hoped that this exploration would help the students recognize the resources they had for supporting their home reading (see Figure 4).

Figure 4 Who Helps Students Read Magazines at Home?

Dad	2	Mum	9
Mum & Dad	14	Uncle	2
Brother	2	Sister	1
Nanna	1		

I was amazed to see the high number of both parents helping the students read because I had assumed the largest number would be for mothers. This gave me additional information about my students' cultural capital. I could now include fathers when talking about reading at home.

I wanted to see the strategies students were using, which would also increase their awareness of the elements of magazines, so I asked the following question:

When you read a magazine, what do you look at first?

Figure 5 reflects the work we had done with magazines.

Figure 5 What Do You Look at First in a Magazine ?

contents	12	news	1
pictures	8	looking through	1
writing	1	dogs & babies	1

I suspect they said "contents" because it was focused on, and they would have said "pictures" before the magazine was explored explicitly.

I then wanted the students to reflect on other useful strategies to help them work through magazine text:

How would you help someone who didn't know how to read a magazine?

They responded:

- Help them spell out words.
- Say the words.
- I'll read it to them.
- Help them with the words.
- I'd ask them to repeat what I say.
- I'd show them the pictures and the magazine too.
- Help them to look at the contents page.
- Use the pictures.
- I don't know.

These diverse responses showed some growth. Although some students did not see the difference between reading a magazine and reading a book, some identified specific and appropriate strategies such as using the contents page, reading the magazine with someone, and using the pictures. In groups, the students identified the important components of a magazine:

news items	crosswords	puzzles
stories	games	Find-a-Word
recipes	photos	phone numbers
addresses	contents page	advertisements
articles	jokes	

These were posted on a chart that proved particularly useful when making our magazine. The students referred to this list many times. The students, again in small groups, answered the question

> Could you read a magazine, then tell someone what it is about without looking at the words?

They responded that "Yes you could, because you can gain meaning by looking at the pictures." Students also identified that "you can't do this with a book."

I now had a clear understanding about what the students had learned, the strategies they used, their preferences for different texts, and the components they used now. Previously, my range of scaffolding strategies for students' reading had been confined to fiction texts, and I had neglected the wide variety of texts children read at home. It was clear that students need different strategies if they are to successfully read and comprehend a diverse range of texts. When writing, children need to know the different structures, elements, and strategies for writing in the different genres.

The Classroom as a Publishing Room

I knew that the students needed hands-on experience creating their own magazines for them to learn how magazines are put together. Therefore, the classroom would become a publishing room for magazines. In our publishing room, the children worked in groups writing different sections for the magazine. Each student contributed an item for each section. There was an air of excitement like that of a publishing room of a commercial magazine—the students moved around the room with purpose and direction.

Baskets were labeled by the students for each section of the magazine: News Items, Stories, Crosswords, Games and Puzzles, and Contents Page. The baskets were the focal point of the activity. When work was completed, it was placed in the appropriate basket. When students, in pairs or individually, were given the task of planning a magazine page, they read the different contributions from the appropriate basket to select a range for that page. This led them to appreciate others' contributions. To ensure that each page was like that of a commercially produced magazine, the students read their selections to one another and asked for feedback about their suitability. There was frequent praise among the students, and visitors to the class were requested to read contributions.

In my years of teaching, I had never seen such a spirit of collaboration and mutual appreciation.

Much of the writing for the magazine took place during National Schools Network[2] time, and two support people were funded by the Network to help in the class. There were other factors that helped in writing the magazine:

- My student teacher moved from group to group and helped students to clarify what they wanted.
- The labeled baskets that sorted the writing gave a framework for the magazine.
- Students took keen interest because they had ownership.
- Students worked independently.
- Students displayed initiative and read all the contributions in order to choose the correct articles for the layout of the pages they were editing.
- Students worked collaboratively, supporting one another and combining their writing.
- Students were willing to make choices.

An important factor in students working collaboratively was their realization that their work needed to be shared with others if they were to create an effective magazine page. They read one another's work and came to appreciate and question other writers.

A Cohesive, Productive Classroom

All the students were focused and enjoyed publishing the *Teddy Magazine*. They wanted to work on it through recess and lunch. The students worked so diligently that we published a second *Teddy Magazine*. During the magazine venture, students stayed on task and cooperated. They had a positive attitude toward the task and one another. There was a supportive, warm, learning environment. The most important result was students' increased confidence.

> *This was a turning point for my class and me. Together we had discovered talents not brought forth before. Other staff members were astonished by the change of energy and attitudes toward learning in my classroom.*

Teaching Implications for Me

In the future I will value the reading material that students bring for reading time. I will encourage them to bring their home texts to class. Silent reading time, which has always been a special time in our classroom, will be more varied, providing for different types of texts for different days. Students will have free choice, but I will promote a different text type of reading each day:

Monday	Fiction books
Tuesday	Nonfiction books
Wednesday	Magazines
Thursday	Comics
Friday	Joke or riddle books/raps and rhymes

We also decided to publish a comic book in the future, which we are very excited about. I have learned to value students' input and to look at the range of texts they bring from home. In the future, I will reflect on my teaching practice, look for hidden assumptions, and try to use explicit teaching techniques and strategies.

Writing a magazine helped students build confidence and take risks. They had the opportunity to become innovative and creative and to explore different ways of publishing. Reluctant writers became eager to write. Students were keen to share their work with peers, other teachers, and the principal. They also were eager to show parents their magazine contributions and write contributions at home. Most importantly, students worked both collaboratively and independently. The students were now set for success, because they knew how to read magazines using components and layout, which was revealed in their writing samples in their reporting folder.

These are the most important lessons I have learned:

- Never underestimate students' capabilities.
- Work within the context of students' understandings.
- Continue to build on cultural capital by valuing home literacies.
- Make explicit the elements of texts so that students can produce them successfully.

I now know that students need explicit guidance. I realize I should not assume or devalue what students do, say, and think, nor make assumptions about their prior knowledge.

References

Carrington, V., & Luke, A. (1997). Literacy and Bourdieu's sociological theory: A reframing. *Language and Education, 11*(2), 96–112.

Freebody, P., Ludwig, C., & Gunn, S. (1995). Everyday literacy practices in and out of schools. In *Children's Literacy National Project* (Vol. 1, pp. 297–315). Adelaide, SA: Department of Education, Employment, and Training.

Notes

[1] Contextualized Learning used in a project called English Language Acquisition, emphasizes the social context of the learning. The teacher and students develop shared goals for the learning, negotiating how they will reach those goals, and building onto the skills and understandings that the students bring to school. The approach is documented in the book, *Supporting English Acquisition* (1994), written by the Aboriginal Education Unit in Adelaide and published by DECS.

[2] The National Schools Network is a school reform network driven by schools with the objective of improving teaching and learning for all Australian students. Schools who join the Network are willing to reform their schools, redesign their work, and change classroom practice to ensure continuous improvement in teaching and learning. Commonwealth funding is provided to set up collaborative classrooms and to provide extra support personnel to work with students with a focus on literacy and writing. To ensure maximum learning, teachers continually assess children's work and meet to plan and evaluate the program.

Chapter Five

Explicit Processes and Strategies Using Literature Circles

Sally Ahang

Sally Ahang, an experienced teacher, spent the first term in her new school finding out about her students as readers and learners. At the same time, she was reading all she could find about literature circles. She had determined the most pressing goals for her students as readers and had concluded that they could reach those goals using literature circles. She devised a way of introducing literature circles to the students so that they would have no doubts as to what was expected of them in classroom reading time, and they would feel supported in the new program.

For the research project, she set specific objectives for her students' reading, and the indicators of achieving those objectives. She made the procedures for the literature circles as explicit as possible by providing clear lists of their options, and by giving each student proformas on which to record their decisions and accomplishments each day in their circles.

In my new school in a low-income area, I had a Years 6 and 7 class of 28 students, ages 11 to 13. The class was in a six-teacher unit, with three other Years 6 and 7 classes. My first term was a period of orientation, during which my reading program focused on accessing nonfiction texts to research, fiction texts including an Australian author, and sustained silent reading (SSR). Several points quickly became obvious during the focus on fiction:

- The students had difficulty selecting texts they could enjoy.
- A large majority of students preferred and selected books from the *Goosebumps* series (Stine) or comics and magazines as reading material.

- They found tasks with long timelines difficult to handle.
- They hated SSR time, which was an expectation across the whole unit.
- Only two students mentioned reading as a hobby in a reader-profile survey.
- Students' oral or written responses displayed an extremely limited critical interaction with texts. Usually they simply retold events.
- Students gave very limited support for any opinions they expressed.

While I agonized over these issues, I had a conversation with a colleague who had used literature circles. She shared some very useful articles (DECS, 1995; Keefe, 1996; Willson & Simpson, 1994), which set out how to get started. At this point, I felt that this strategy could work for me and could offer my students improved reading experiences and outcomes.

Literature circles are a means of setting up a collaborative and social experience of reading. By splitting the class into groups of four to six students and giving each group a different novel to read, a class could have as many as four or five novels to read and discuss. This is not a return to the old round-robin, whole-class reading experience. This is a much more exciting strategy.

Just how collaborative the literature circles activity becomes is up to the teacher and the students. There is potential for students to negotiate the selection, planning, reading, discussion, and follow-up reading. The opportunity for a critical community to develop among the groups of students is challenging to facilitate: What did I want? What did I do? And what happened? There were four main outcomes I was aiming for, and the Table on pages 51–52 sets out the strategies and resources used to reach these outcomes and the indicators that would show that I had reached the outcomes.

What Did I Want?

The planning table was crucial in setting up my direction. I had never planned so thoroughly before and the results showed. Because I knew which indicators to look for and reinforce in the literature circles, I could be more specific in giving feedback and could see which aspects required teaching.

What Did I Do?

1. I identified what my students needed, and I set goals to meet those needs.
2. I found out more about literature circles. I read articles, talked with others who had tried them, and identified the essential elements—

TABLE   Expected Outcomes of Literature Circles

What students know, understand, or can do	Indicators	Helpful aids, resources, and strategies
• Reading is an active and interactive process/task	• students talk freely about what they're reading • increased interaction on discussion sessions • the types of questions and statements used in discussion and response writing • the number of questions and comments that go beyond retelling the story	• critical questions chart • sentence starters • monitoring sheet for contributions made • Bloom's taxonomy (McGrath & Noble, 1996) • training and development materials for gifted students • audio cassette recorder • monitoring sheet with space to put teacher comments or record student responses
• Different people can have different opinions and understanding of the same text	• students accept contributions of others without put downs • establish rules and a Y chart for effective discussion • students piggy-back on ideas of others • students' contributions are in response to others' ideas	• focus initial discussion on the richness of a diverse community • modelling process • brainstorm possible responses, e.g., "I hadn't thought of that" "You're right...and I also think...," "Can you tell me a bit more about that so I can understand what you're saying?"
• Students make thoughtful and critical comments on reading	• the amount of retelling decreases, and the amount of talk focused on critical thinking and interaction with the text and author's style and intentions increases • types of questions asked	• monitoring sheet • audio cassette recorder

continued

TABLE   Planned Outcomes of Literature Circles (continued)

What students know, understand, or can do	Indicators	Helpful aids, resources, and strategies
• Students can write a critical review or response incorporating opinions supported by comments by teacher references to the text	• content of written responses • specific and comprehensive feedback • content of sticky notes • sticky notes for recording	• written response books • modelling process • drafting/ conferencing process • ongoing thoughts and questions

what worked well and what did not. I compiled a range of strategies for what to do and adapted and modified the ideas to suit the goals of me and my students.

3. I uncovered more about my students' interests. They completed a reader's profile (inventory) that gave me information about the students' attitudes and experiences with reading. They also completed a learning-preference checklist based on Gardner's "multiple intelligences" (as cited in McGrath & Noble, 1996), which helped me identify areas of strength that students could bring to reading circles. I discussed with students last term's reading program and how they felt about it. We then developed a list of effective reader behaviors and skills, which identified for students the elements they needed to be more effective readers.

4. I found books to match the students' interests. I checked the school's resource center for available multiple copies. I made the initial selection because of my concern with students' selection skills. I chose 10 titles to introduce to the students using the information they had provided plus my own observations. Included were books by Emily Rodda, Roy Pond, and Gillian Rubinstein. I read the blurbs and skimmed each book to get a feel for it. I would read particular books more thoroughly if specific student groups needed more guid-ed support.

As the students used the books, I discovered that my selections held little appeal for students. I, therefore, had to promote each title enthusiastically. I have since played a larger role in the school's purchase of books for discussion groups. To do this, I tune in to students' spontaneous responses to titles.

5. I planned and produced several sheets to support the literature-circles process (see figures throughout chapter).

Introducing the Novels and Creating the Groups

I first explained literature circles to the class. Their first step was to identify books they wanted to read and discuss. I introduced each novel by reading the blurb, making general comments, and inviting students who had read any of the books to add their comments. I kept these introductions brief and distributed a handout (see Figure 1) on which the students recorded their first, second, and third preferences. This sheet helped focus students' selection and was the means to forming groups. On the basis of their preferences, I formed seven groups, four people to a group. All students were placed in a group with their first or second preference. The groups were an interesting mix of students and added an unpredictable element.

I distributed a reading checklist (see Figure 2) of the activities for each week, which we went over together. The original cycle was 6 weeks, with the final written response and presentation completed in the sixth week. This could be adapted for more or less weeks depending on the length of the books, the students' reading speeds, and the time available for literature circles. The students asked a lot of clarifying questions. At this point, I realized that the students' ideas of the process was different than mine. My idea was for groups to meet once a week for discussion of their book with me sitting in. The students' idea, on the other hand, was more group oriented—with them meeting in groups every day.

FIGURE 1   Student Selection Sheet

READING CIRCLES

Name:_____

1st preference_____

2nd preference_____

3rd preference_____

FIGURE 2 Reading Checklist

	Week 1	Week 2	Week 3	Week 4	Week 5	Week 6
Reached agreed reading target page (written in box)						
Sticky notes completed						
Written this week's response						
Participated in discussion circle						
Handed up reading response book for marking						

Final response completed

Presentation

Because this was my first attempt at literature circles, I did not know what was going to work, so I let the groups operate as they were as long as they kept within the framework of weekly activities that I had set. Time set aside each day to read, discuss, or write worked well. This was literature circles time. Each group divided their time differently. Some sat together and read silently, then discussed for the last 5 minutes; some read in turn and discussed as they went along; others formed groups and read to a designated page, then came back together to discuss. They became adept at judging their time. I was pleased that I let them decide how to operate within groups.

The students designed and made a special cover for their reading response book. They pasted the reading checklist into their reading response exercise book and recorded basic organizational information for the first reading cycle (see Figure 3). Then a weekly timetable was drawn (with a different order for each group), which was structured around each group's discussion day (see Figure 4).

Both sheets oriented the students to a new activity. However, they proved useful for further reading cycles—as a focus for initial decision making, and then for day-to-day operations. Discussion groups were 15 minutes long and were the focus of my role in the week's process. I had two discussion groups on each Monday and Tuesday, and one group on the other three days. This allowed time to catch up with groups that missed their usual discussion time and to touch base with groups in their other circle activities.

Prior to beginning in groups, I explained the purpose of the sticky notes and demonstrated their use. Each student was given several, which were used to record questions and comments about specific parts of the story shared and also to record links made to their own lives and experiences (see Figure 5). At first, some students went overboard with their sticky notes. With time and prompting, they were used more

FIGURE 3   Basic Organizational Information for Each Reading Cycle

Novel: _____

Author: _____

People in my group: _____

Discussion day: _____

Written response day: _____

FIGURE 4   Weekly Timetable

Monday	Tuesday	Wednesday	Thursday	Friday
• Reading and add sticky notes • Write points	• Reading with sticky notes • Select new target page to bring up	• Discussion with teacher • Jot down ideas shared in discussion	• Written response	• Reading with sticky notes

FIGURE 5 Examples of Sticky Notes

sparingly. Some groups stopped using the notes altogether after reaching a spot in their book where they were more interested in what was coming next. Again, allowing for variability was an advantage.

The groups collected their novels and selected a working area. They decided how they would like to work in the daily half-hour literature circle. A range of working styles emerged as students gained a level of comfort and trust within their groups. Some decided to sit in groups, but read silently; some chose to read around the circle, but agreed you could pass if you wanted to; some chose to read at their desks and convened their group only at agreed points in their reading or if a member raised a question; and some read silently on some days and together on other days.

A rule was made about books going back into their storage box between circle times and books were not to be taken home. An exception was made if a student had been absent or needed to catch up to meet the target page established by the group. In this way, most groups completed a novel in 4 to 5 weeks. This time could be reduced if SSR time was used in addition to circle time for reading.

After completing the novel, the students were allowed 1 week to write a final written response to the novel and present an activity. As we progressed toward the final week, I demonstrated using joint construction how to use the Paragraph Planning Sheet (see Figure 6 on the next page).

FIGURE 6   Paragraph Planning Sheet

Name _____   Date _____

PLANNING and ORGANIZING WRITING

Focus of paragraph	Dot point list of my ideas	Extra ideas from a critical friend
1. Introduce the book generally	• title, author • characters – Russell, Dr. Chen, children children snoop around his house, the children's discoveries. • settings – bus stop, house, school yard, ice hockey arena.	• Did this author write any other books?

2. My likes and dislikes about the book	• likes • dislikes
	  – mystery created – hardly any action
	  – interesting to – story doesn't
	    find out about match my
	    Dr. Chen's life expectations
	  – Dr. Chen's – last ¼ gets
	    character boring; author's
	            writing style.
		• What were you expecting when you chose this book?
		• Do you only enjoy action books?

3. Author's style of writing and message	• Message: Don't judge a book by its cover or what they're doing.
	• two different parts of the storyline don't fit together well
	• mystery in middle part of story
	  – is he or isn't he a vampire?
	  – looking through windows and making judgments.	

4. Comments and recommendations	• recommend it to younger readers • plot boring • storyline needed some changes • characters sometimes realistic and sometimes not. • narrator used—don't really like it.	• Would you read another story by this author?

In a writing lesson, we identified a topic and brainstormed ideas related to the topic. We looked for connections between the ideas and grouped them on the chalkboard. Each student decided on four groups of ideas he or she wanted to write about. They used the Paragraph Planning Sheet to label each paragraph in the left column and to write in dot points the related ideas in the second column (selecting a preferred order). Then with a friend they shared their written ideas and how they were organized. The partner's ideas were added in the third column. They were ready to write their four paragraphs, and the sheet was introduced as part of a writing topic. The students had plenty to write about. Most were able to apply the process to their final written

FIGURE 7   Final Written Book Response

book response (see Figure 7) without difficulty. The structure was used frequently for all sorts of writing throughout the year.

The activities were introduced to the whole class at a later date, and the list of final presentation activities was explained (see Figure 8). The chosen activities tended to be those that were familiar to the class. To increase the range of choices, I modeled and scaffolded some of the less familiar. With groups completing their activities at different times, I provided other activities to fill the gap until the cycle of literature circles was completed.

FIGURE 8 Final Presentation Activities

- Design a labeled character poster.
- Draw a story map.
- Build a stand-up model of a character.
- Create a new book cover using your favorite part of the story.
- Develop a crossword puzzle about the book.
- Write a quiz card and answer sheet.
- Paint a painting of a pivotal point in the story.
- Make a mobile using a branch or a coat hanger.
- Dramatize part of the story.
- Make up a song that summarizes the story or a character's development through the story.
- Make a diorama that shows an exciting, unhappy, or mysterious event in the book.
- Practice reading an extract to read aloud to the class. Include different voices and sound effects.

Monitoring Students' Participation

I joined a discussion group and placed myself where I had a clear view of all the groups. On the Teacher's Monitoring Sheet (see Figure 9), I recorded students' participation and what this demonstrated they could do as readers. The students were always keen to have this information fed back to them. After the first few observations, I showed them my record, and we discussed the types of participation I had observed. We talked about good examples they had demonstrated and practiced any that were underrepresented.

When I first used the monitoring sheet, I reflected on the types of responses I was looking for. For example, *Responding* meant others' comments and *Initiating* meant introducing a new topic. I considered deleting *Listening* as all the other categories include this.

Explicit Processes and Strategies Using Literature Circles   **59**

FIGURE 9 Teacher's Monitoring Sheet

STUDENTS' NAMES OBSERVED Novel				Week			STUDENTS' NAMES OBSERVED Novel				Week			
Listening							Listening							
Responding							Responding							
Questioning							Questioning							
Clarifying							Clarifying							
Initiating							Initiating							
Comment							Comment							

Adapted from Simpson, A. (1995). *Working with literature texts in small groups*. Adelaide, SA: Department of Education and Children's Services.

What Was Achieved?

By the end of a book cycle, I had at least four monitoring sheets for each group. An analysis of the data revealed the following:

- All children but one had participated equally,
- Listening, clarifying, and responding occurred at a consistently high level in all groups,
- There were differences in what the groups focused on in their discussions and in the kinds of support they needed from me.

These sheets and my observations led me to conclude that the literature circles strategy will be an integral part of my program. It offered my students many opportunities to develop as learners and critical thinkers:

- The students shared personal experiences that linked with the texts, sorted out misunderstandings, interpreted philosophical questions, clarified meanings of words, and argued about the authors' craft.
- They persevered with a text that might otherwise have been abandoned within a few pages.

- The social structure and experience of reading in literature circles helped the students to enjoy and value a broader range of literature.
- The discussions about books brought about new insights, expressions of feelings, learning from one another, and the motivation to read.
- Students, who had been unsuccessful with reading experiences previously, made significant progress with this strategy. They actually enjoyed themselves.

Through observing and monitoring these literature circles, I learned a great deal about what the students did as they were reading: their thoughts, how they made meaning, and how their misunderstandings came about. I had never had these insights during previous author studies. I realized how my previous choices of activities had severely restricted the opportunities for students to show me what they could do.

Future Directions

I plan to run a cycle of literature circles each term with my Years 6 and 7 class. This leaves 4 or 5 weeks to focus on other strategies that highlight different aspects of becoming an effective reader.

Two main priorities in developing literature circles in the future are to investigate strategies to utilize students' thinking skills in a variety of ways when tackling texts, and to develop my own insights and understandings of what is commonly referred to as the "author's style." There is still much learning to be done, and I look forward to that in my next literature circles.

References

Department of Education and Children's Services. Working with literature texts in small groups. (1995). In *Texts: The heart of the curriculum* (No. 4). Adelaide, SA: Author.

Keefe, C.H. (1996). Literature Circles: Reducing reading stress. *Reading, 3(3)*.

McGrath, H., & Noble, T. (1996). *Seven ways at once. Classroom strategies based on the seven intelligences*. Melbourne, VIC: Addison Wesley Longman Australia.

Stine, R.L. Goosebumps series. New York: Scholastic.

Willson, P., & Simpson, A. (1994). Literature circles: Children reading, writing and talking about literature. *The Literature Base*, June, 9–12.

Chapter Six

What's Happening in Your Reading Program?

Kerry Gehling

Kerry Gehling plans her teaching of literacy around a theme. For her research project, she built her reading program around the students' production based on T.S. Eliot's (1939) poems about cats. Some of the skills she focused on such as reading fluently and reading with expression were directly related to the production, while other skills and understandings were selected because they were ones the students were lacking and ready to learn. However, the activities devised to teach these skills and understandings—the role of diagrams in information texts and illustrations in picture books, and the selection of main points—were only loosely connected with the cats theme.

As part of her explicit-teaching research, Kerry sought to extend her intention to make clear to her Year 7 students and their parents the purposes, activities, and assessment of their learning. She was motivated by parents' lack of understanding about the focus of her reading program. Kerry reported how she made her teaching explicit to her students and how the reading goals, activities, and related student achievements were communicated to parents. A questionnaire sent to parents revealed how well they had understood the communications and their reactions to the reading program.

S eated on the playground equipment early one morning, a parent shared her concerns about her 10-year-old child's reading. During the discussion, I concluded that although she had a general awareness of the reading program in the classroom, she had not been informed explicitly of the expected outcomes. She looked for improved fluency and word attack as outcomes of a good reading program. Of course, my objectives were much wider. My reading program is structured around the analysis of different texts. I have refined this process over the years and felt pleased about the achievements and enjoyment my students showed in their reading. This parent's comments made me ask the questions that follow:

- How could I be more explicit—not only with the students but with the parents too?

- Was my confidence in students' outcomes reflected in the parents' attitudes?
- What were parents' reactions to my requiring children to work with longer timelines and take more responsibility for their own learning?
- How could I expand parents' ideas about the breadth of reading outcomes in a primary school reading program?

The integrated theme of the program was animals, which was chosen because of the aim to produce and present poems about cats. Both the reading and word study assignments were based on animals, and I chose texts that had some connection with animals. The unit planning map (see Figure 1) for the integrated unit shows how the theme was developed across the curriculum.

Communication With Parents

In our school, we developed a regular system of communication with parents, which included letters, portfolios, and questionnaires. At the beginning of the term, a letter (see Figure 2 on page 65) was sent to parents outlining the reading program and the four objectives to be achieved. In addition, the letter outlined ways parents could support their developing readers and invited them to be part of the reading circle programs by assisting students as they practiced the skills explicitly taught in the lessons. Portfolios were folders with plastic sleeves into which major assessment tasks were inserted. Each assessment task had an outline of the set task and its intended outcomes, an explanation of the learning content, an example of the student's work, and space for teacher, student, and parent comment. Portfolios were to be sent home at least once a term. However, students took them home each time an assessment task was completed so that parents were informed of current work while the students were enthused about it. During the animals unit, portfolios were sent home four times.

The Reading Lessons

Because I was explicit with my students about the features of texts that they needed to learn, it was not difficult to make these aspects explicit to parents. The following objectives that the students needed for research and literature appreciation fit well with the theme and the presentation of T.S. Eliot poems:

1. Identify the role of pictures and illustrations.
2. Interpret and create diagrams.
3. Understand the features of information text.
4. Present choral reading fluently and expressively.

FIGURE 1   Unit Planning Map

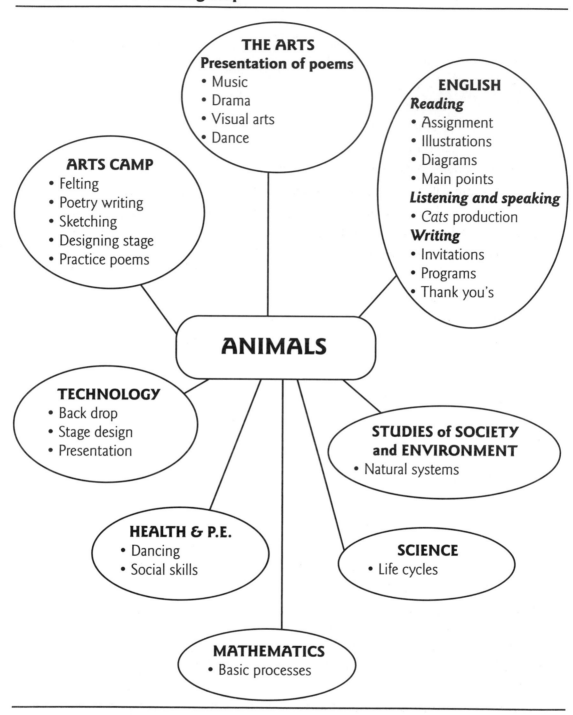

FIGURE 2 Explanatory Letter to Parents

Dear Parents,

The children have been given a reading program for the term which asks them to read a variety of types of books about animals. The specific requirements are:

- Seven books will be read:
    - 2 chapter books
    - 3 picture books
    - 2 information books
- One activity will be completed for each book.
- A record will be kept of the books read—this is a minimum requirement.

I will make the following points explicit in particular lessons. I shall report on these points at the end of the term in the students' portfolios:

- To use pictures to help make meaning from text.
- To read and use a diagram.
- To select main points from an information text.
- To use expression that is appropriate for the text.

The other component of this program is the production based on T.S. Eliot's (1939) *Old Possum's Book of Practical Cats* in which we will do choral reading and practice using appropriate expression. I expect that the more able readers will be able to act as voice leaders in the beginning. As less-confident readers begin to know and remember parts, I will expect them to take a more vocal part in the reading. The repetition will support all readers in word recognition, expression, and performing for an audience.

You can help at home by

- listening to your child read one poem per day,
- once parts have been allocated, listening to your child say his or her parts daily,
- reading to and with your child,
- sharing books,
- helping to ensure that time management of the reading assignment is up to date, and
- showing an interest in the work being done on the reading assignment.

Some parents are donating their time on Tuesday mornings to be part of our Reading Circle Program. A different activity to support the explicit teaching points is completed each week. If you have time available, another two Reading Circle leaders are needed. I have included a comment sheet in the portfolios for leaders' comments about how each child managed the task.

If you have any questions about this program or would like to join us for a lesson at any time, please let me know, or make time for a discussion, remembering that three-way conferences are just around the corner.

Regards to you all.

Each of these four objectives was taught in a set of lessons and included the learning and assessment tasks for the students. The work assessed for each objective, with comments, was sent home to parents to inform them of the learning content and the expectations, and to show examples of students' work for each objective.

Objective 1: Identify the Role of Pictures and Illustrations

Lesson 1: The Role of Pictures and Illustrations

I asked and we discussed the question "What is a picture book?" I read aloud to the class some picture books that were chosen for the different ways they use pictures:

Window, by Jeannie Baker, is a story told only in pictures.

Crocodile Beat, by Gail Jorgensen, is a story in which the pictures flow with the words and add a twist at the end where the words are not interpreted literally.

Just Another Ordinary Day, by Rod Clements, provides an ordinary text with wildly imaginative pictures that change the interpretation markedly.

Mufaro's Beautiful Daughters: An African Tale, by John Steptoe, is a story in which text and pictures flow well together—pictures elaborate and add meaning to the text.

After each reading, we discussed how the illustrations add to the meaning of the text, which resulted in a charted list of features.

The students were fascinated by how much there was to discover in illustrations—they had thought they were past picture books.

Lesson 2: Students in Pairs

Students formed pairs and read a picture book, which they chose, to a partner, and explained how the pictures added to the text. Partners then wrote letters thanking the other for their reading and explanation and gave feedback on how well they were understood. Students referred to the charted list of features produced in Lesson 1. However, interactive trouble (see Preface, p. vii) occurred because I was not explicit about the explanation being the primary task. The students did not go into detail about how the pictures were used, which made the letter-writing task more difficult. Because the students had not fully understood my requirements, I realized that I must be clearer in my explanations. I then demonstrated the explanation requirement using a book.

Lesson 3: Explain in Groups

In reading groups, students shared picture books and explained to group members how the pictures added to the text. Again, they referred to the charted list from Lesson 1.

Lesson 4: Assessment

The students were asked to answer the following question in writing: In what ways can pictures help with the understanding of text?

FIGURE 3   Student Work Sample

★ Pictures can help the text by changing the meaning of words like saying cat and showing lion.

★ Pictures can help the text by illustrating the story without words

★ Pictures can help the text by changing the meaning of words only at the end of the story. For ex: In Crocodile beat the picture matches all the story in the begining but not in the end.

★ Pictures can help the text by explaning the words more clearly like matching all the words in picture.

All the students' answers showed a good understanding of the relation between pictures and text (see Figure 3 and 4). Although the charted list was removed, the four books that illustrated uses remained on display. Most students wrote about four ways that pictures add meaning to text as had been listed. The student's work sample in

FIGURE 4 Assessment for Student Portfolio

Pictures can contribute to a story in different ways:

- Pictures that tell the complete story without any text, e.g., *Window* by Jeannie Baker
- Pictures that add a twist to the end of the end of the story by changing the meaning of the text at the end, e.g., *Crocodile Beat* by Gail Jorgensen, illustrated by Patricia Mullins
- Pictures that change the whole meaning of the story, e.g., *Just Another Ordinary Day* by Rod Clement
- Pictures that match the text, illustrating the words literally, e.g., *Mufaro's Beautiful Daughters: An African Tale* by John Steptoe

These stories have been read and discussed. Students have worked out how the illustrations are used to support the text. The assessment asks them to elaborate their understandings.

> **Teacher comment**
>
> An excellent explaination Tapaswi. You show that you have an excellent understanding of the different uses.

> **Student comment**
>
> I enjoyed reading Window, Crocodile Beat, Just Another Ordinary Day and Mufaro's Daughters. I was able to understand in what ways pictures can help the text by reading those books. I think I did very well in the task.

> **Parent comment**
>
> Tapaswi, Excellent! I feel you are learning very well. 24/7/19

Figure 3 shows in her own words these four ways. The comment sheet that accompanied the student's work listed the charted roles of illustrations.

The charted features list developed in Lesson 1 was used by the students without any prompting. After one term using feature lists, the students used them with confidence.

Objective 2: Interpret and Create Diagrams

Lesson 1: Charted List

The class discussed a book containing animal diagrams with all the animals' parts labeled. I elicited the elements of a diagram and charted the list. We read a diagram as a class and recorded the information found. Each student was given a photocopied diagram and asked to read and record what could be learned from it. This activity made students more aware of the make up of a diagram, and they had more ownership of what was required.

Lesson 2: Reading Circle

In reading circles, the students read another diagram and answered questions:

- What is the purpose of the diagram?
- How can you tell that this is a diagram?
- Write three interesting facts learned by reading this diagram.
- List words to be discussed to help you understand their meaning or pronunciation.
- Would it be easier to understand the diagram information if it were written in a paragraph? Explain.

One student from each group then reported back to the class.

Lesson 3: Drawing

As part of the word study assignment, students drew a diagram of an animal.

Lesson 4: Assessment

Students listed the criteria for a diagram (see Figure 5) and explained why diagrams are helpful when reading information texts. Once assessed and I had written a comment, this task was added to their portfolios, along with an assessment explanation

FIGURE 5   Student Work Sample of Criteria for a Diagram

*Title ✓
*Picture-usually drawn
* Labels ✓

Explain why diagrams are very helpful when reading some information texts.

1. They make comparisons easier ✓
2. They help you understand some imformation better ✓
3. They can show you how things work ✓
4. They can show you things you couldn't normally see ✓

(see Figure 6 on page 71), the student's comment, and an invitation for a comment from parents.

Most students showed a clear understanding of a diagram and how it can help in reading information texts. They were particularly successful in using diagrams and interested in working with them. I plan to include students' use of their own diagrams in future units and assessments.

Objective 3: Main Points From Information Texts

Lesson 1: Topic Sentences

I introduced the idea of topic sentences. With the librarian's assistance, students found topic sentences in information books, and learned that the topic sentence is the first sentence in a paragraph and can be used in note taking.

FIGURE 6   Assessment of Diagrams for Student Portfolio

Outcomes
- Students are able to identify what a diagram is and how it can be used to find information.
- Students understand how a diagram can add to the text in which it is located.

Teacher's comment
Students were shown a book that contains many diagrams, and the class brainstormed what criteria make up a diagram. We decided on the following criteria:
- a title
- a picture, which is usually drawn rather than photographed
- the picture is labeled, usually with pointers to show what the label refers to

The children as a group showed enjoyment in working with diagrams and found that they were easy to find information from. Some students were a little unsure of how the text and diagram go together and needed to give this some thought.

I have included a personal comment on the assessment worksheet.

Student's comment

I found that if there is a diagram it is easy to understand what it is and where it is. I think I did very well in diagrams but it's quite hard to draw a diagram.

Parent's comment

Tapaswi,

Your diagram was nice. And you learned very useful important topics too.

24/7/97

Lesson 2: Read and Report Main Points

In reading circles with parents, students read and discussed a newspaper article. They reported orally the main point to the class.

Lesson 3: Class Work With Big Books

Students read three nonfiction Big Books as a class:

Whale Rap by Joan Van Bramer and Janine Scott (1992)
Volcanoes by Bernie Joyce (1992)
Mem: An Autobiography by Mem Fox (1993)

They selected the topic sentences from *Whale Rap*. They then selected the main point from each page of *Volcanoes* and put it in their own words. Before opening the autobiography, *Mem*, students made a list of questions about the book. They answered their questions by reading the book and listing any questions that required further research. These were children's books, so main points were found easily. From then on they researched with confidence.

Lesson 4: Assessment

Students were asked to complete two tasks:

1. Read a text about feral cats and complete the following:
   - Where will you look for the topic sentences in information text?
   - List the main points in the text about feral cats in your own words (see Figure 7).

2. Read a one-page profile about Patricia Mullins, a children's book illustrator, and complete the following:
   - List questions you have about Patricia Mullins.
   - Read and make notes from reading the text to answer your questions.
   - Make a list of questions that need further research.

Most of the students identified the topic sentence and listed main points in their own words. Some students had difficulty reading particular words, which I helped them with by pronouncing and explaining the meaning. The students circled these words to identify them for their portfolios. Another difficulty I identified in the main points assignment was a differing interpretation of the text, producing a slightly skewed understanding. As a class, we reread the text and discussed the main points, which clarified these problems. Without further guidance the students completed their research tasks about an illustrator (see Figure 8 on page 74). They had developed and answered their own questions and planned their summary.

The assessment sheet (see Figure 9 on page 75) listed the intended outcomes and included comments by me, the teacher, and the student and made provision for parent comments.

FIGURE 7   Finding Main Points in Information Text

1. Where will you look for the topic sentences in information text?

In the first sentence of a paragraph.   ✓

2. List the main points, in your own words, from this writing about Feral Cats.

★ Some cats living in the wild are domestic cats whom(which) are dumped by their owners.   ✓

★ Feral cats are found all around the Australia.   ✓

★ Scientists have discovered that the most feral cats are either tabby or ginger.   ✓

★ Scientists say that black, black and (and)white cats are easily seen by predators and they are also easily seen by smaller animals which cats try to hunt.   ✓

FIGURE 8   Research Strategy

① List the questions you would like to find the answers to about Patricia Mullins.

• Where and when born?
Born in Balwyn, Victoria

• How old was she when she first started to illustrate books?
When She was 18

• Is she married? Does she have any children? She has a 12 year old
She is married
• Where does she live?
Fitzroy, Victoria

• Does she have any pets?
When she was young she had lots and a dog Called Ricky

② Read the text and make notes to answer your questions.

③ On the back of this sheet List any questions you would need to do further research to find answers for.

FIGURE 9   Assessment Sheet

READING

Information Text: Outcomes

1. To be aware that the topic sentence is usually the first sentence in a paragraph and to use this knowledge to select the main points from a piece of information text.

2. To use the research strategy of...
   - listing questions to be asked about a selected topic
   - reading to find answers to these questions and recording answers in own words
   - listing any remaining questions for further research

Teacher comment

This shows good research skills Joanna. You have written your points clearly.

Student comment

Finding the main points in a piece of writing can be very hard sometimes. This was one of the hardest pieces of work I have done all year.

Parent comment

Its' good to see these valuable skills being taught at year 5 level, and to see that Joanna found the work challenging enough to extend her.

What's Happening in Your Reading Program

Objective 4: Appropriate Expression

There were two primary objectives for our work with the poems of T.S. Eliot:

- To be able to read poems to a group in an expressive and interesting voice.
- To be able to improve oral reading ability with the use of a supportive environment and the goal of performance.

In the beginning, the more able readers would act as voice leaders. As the readers with less confidence began to know and remember parts, they took greater and more vocal part in the reading. Repeated readings supported all readers in word recognition, expression, and performing for an audience. Parents assisted by listening to one poem per day, and listening to individual parts often.

Lesson Sequence

1. The poems were read aloud to the class, and the students joined in as they felt confident.
2. Each poem was given to a group of students who practiced it reading aloud, often supported by a parent. The students were encouraged to give one another feedback about clarity, expression, and pace.
3. The poems were then practiced without words, and students memorized them.
4. With the support of an adult when needed, the groups made suggestions about staging and props, and volunteers were called for the different parts.
5. The whole class made suggestions and negotiated how the poems would be presented.
6. The students then practiced the poems as a dramatic presentation, with gestures, staging, and movement.
7. A weekend camp was organized to polish the whole presentation.
8. The class presented the poems to two school audiences and one parent audience.

Assessment

After the performance, summary sheets of students' achievements in all curriculum areas involved with the theme were completed and placed in their learning portfolios (see Figure 10 on page 77).

FIGURE 10   Summary Sheet of Student Achievement

"CATS"

ENGLISH

Speaking & Listening

Outcomes

★★✔To speak with understanding of character, mood, and setting.

★★✔To speak to a large audience with confidence.

★★✔To listen and respond within the setting to portray a character.

Reading

Outcomes

★★✔Explores character, mood, and setting through choral reading.

★★✔Shows understanding of classical narrative poems.

★★✔Develops fluency and expression in oral reading and widens vocabulary.

STUDENT COMMENT I think my reading has improved this year. So has my speaking and listening. Cats made me alot more confident about speaking in front of an audience.

TEACHER COMMENT
Excellent work Joanna. You showed, not only great performance skills, but also a good understanding of the poems and the characters they portray.

PARENT COMMENT
The group read beautifully and we enjoyed seeing her as part of it. She studiously learned the lines at home, and thoroughly enjoyed the challenge of working in a different register and with the broad, rich vocabulary in the poems. Joanna's, and the whole group's, characterization was excellent.

Outcomes in each area were marked as being achieved (a check), achieved well (one star), or outstanding achievement (two stars). Teacher and student comments were added, and space was provided for parent comment.

Student Achievement

The presentation was greatly enjoyed by the performers and audience alike. Confidence developed markedly and students showed greater willingness to try reading unfamiliar text and present themselves to an audience. Students were very positive in their reviews, and many parents made glowing comments about their children's achievements. The repetitions and joint decision making meant that all students achieved at a high standard and felt proud of it. In addition, parents and peers reinforced the students' achievement with high praise.

Parent Questionnaire and Comments

To find out how much the parents had gained from the different communications to them and about their involvement in aspects of the program, a questionnaire with five questions was sent home:

1. In what ways do you feel that this program has helped your child in his or her reading?
2. Were the outcomes clearly explained in the portfolio proformas?
3. Is there anything you would like to change about them?
4. Do these outcomes meet your expectations about what your child will be taught in reading at school?
5. What would you like to see addressed to strengthen your child's reading?

Parent Comments

- I feel Thomas is much more confident and enjoys reading more.
- I have seen a great improvement in Michelle's understanding of what she is reading. She is putting more expression into the stories.
- Broadened her [reading] material. Highlighted that reading books has many different uses, i.e., pleasure, reference, and information.
- The program has helped Annalise to read more different types of stories, especially poems. It was useful in highlighting the role of text, pictures, and diagrams.

• I believe that children like William need extra motivation to read. Reading activities such as these give purpose to his reading other than just for fun or just because he has to.

Final Reflections

This was a very full, exciting, and profitable term's work. The students became a cohesive group. They enjoyed learning, knew they had been successful in their achievements, and knew they had come a long way in their learning and in taking responsibility for their learning.

References

Eliot, T.S. (1939). *Old Possum's book of practical cats*. London: Faber and Faber.
Fox, M. (1993). *Mem: An autobiography*. Adelaide, SA: Era Publications.
Joyce, B. (1992). *Volcanoes*. Sydney, NSW: Bookshelf.
Van Bramer, J., & Scott, J. (1992). *Whale rap*. Auckland, New Zealand: Shortland Publications.

Children's Literature References

Baker, J. (1991). *Window*. New York: Greenwillow.
Clements, R. (1997). *Just another ordinary day*. HarperCollins.
Jorgensen, G., & Mullins, P. (1994). *Crocodile beat*. New York: Simon & Schuster
Steptoe, J. (1987). *Mufaro's beautiful daughters: An African tale*. New York: Lothrop.

Chapter Seven

The Aim Is Metacognition: For Teachers as Well as Students

Meredith Edwards

As coordinator of English and literacy at a suburban secondary school, Meredith Edwards and the humanities staff were concerned about monitoring and teaching reading skills to their students. In this school, the English teachers also teach Year 8 classes society and environment, and both subjects share literacy objectives. These secondary teachers were required to record and report students' reading strategies and to teach the strategies even though they had no training in this area.

Meredith recognized that a research project on the explicit teaching of reading complemented another project in which her staff was involved, which focused on using student achievement data to improve students' learning outcomes. In order to collect achievement data in reading, teachers needed to be clear about what skills were involved. Being explicit about the intended outcomes would assist the teachers and the students in reaching those outcomes. Both projects would provide support for the teachers as they sought to be explicit about reading skills.

The approach that Meredith and her staff chose was to agree on a set of reading strategies that their students might use, to provide the students with a list of these strategies, to teach the strategies in both English and society and environment classes, to help the students monitor their use of the strategies in their reading strategies journals, and to keep a checklist of each student's use of those strategies.

The first thing our group of teachers did was to develop a shared working definition of what explicit teaching means. We agreed with South Australian educator Lyn Wilkinson's (author of Chapter I in this volume) definition:

It is about making the hidden obvious; exposing and explaining what is taken for granted; demystifying mental processes; letting children in on the information and strategies which will enable them to become powerful literacy users. (Wilkinson, 1995)

As secondary teachers, we expected students to come to us as competent readers. If they did not, we had the primary teachers to blame, which we knew was not fair, but we put aside such thoughts and structured a range of opportunities for students to read. We read a variety of genres as shared texts, read to and with the classes, and provided opportunities for students to read widely. These schemes were laudable to the extent that we turned on students to reading and encouraged them to extend their interaction with greater ranges of texts. What we were not as proficient doing, though, was describing the reading strategies that our students employed as readers. Neither were many of us comfortable with diagnosing problems that our students encounter in their reading.

Like most secondary teachers throughout South Australia, the English faculty felt daunted initially by the task of attributing reading levels using our state's learning outcomes continuum[1], because most had not received preservice training about how students learn to read. As English teachers, we were particularly concerned with the following questions:

What are we looking for when we observe students as readers?

What assessment tools are available to assist us in measuring student achievement, and what are the advantages and disadvantages of each?

How will we record our observations?

What methodologies best support students in their development as readers?

An additional consideration was that the Year 8 English teachers also taught society and environment classes. In society and environment faculty meetings, our investigation of the set outcomes had also led us to consider how we could support students to develop the appropriate reading skills required of the higher level outcomes illustrated in the investigation, communication, and participation strand. At level 6, midsecondary level, this strand requires students to

- explain various ways of viewing an issue and the information associated with it,
- discuss the logic of and evidence of an argument or viewpoint, and
- come to an informed personal decision through discussing and considering viewpoints and evidence presented by others.

These outcomes matched outcomes in the English curriculum framework at a similar level. Consequently, Year 8 teachers in both faculties decided on a cross-curricular approach to reading.

Help initially arrived in two forms: from the action research into the explicit teaching of reading, and from a departmental project called Using Student Achievement Data to Improve Student Learning Outcomes. The classroom research project into the explicit teaching of reading meshed well with the goals of the outcomes project aimed at using student achievement data to verify the effectiveness of specific classroom practices. Student achievement data would clarify what we needed to teach; being explicit about the outcomes we intended meant we could spell out these for our students and assist our planning for teaching and assessment from the beginning.

Setting Up the Explicit Teaching of Reading Project

The call for explicitness in the teaching, assessment, and reporting of student achievement in the area of reading underlined our need for training and development in this area. A mentor for the projects conducted training and development about explicit teaching along with four teachers of Year 8 society and environment and English and two classroom support teachers who had been released through flexible staffing.

With classes of more than 30 students, we feared that we would not be able to give each student the individual attention required for them to understand the reading strategies. However, having the two support teachers in the classroom helped to encourage students to articulate how they tackled reading demands.

Previous experience had taught us the need for shared training and development, which provided opportunities for extended and ongoing discussions about classroom applications of ideas. Only then are changes to teaching practice and student learning outcomes likely to occur. The Using Student Achievement Data project assisted us by providing temporary teacher cover so that the key teachers could attend training and development sessions on school time, and we were able to meet as a team to discuss progress of the project in each of our four classrooms with our mentor.

Training and Development on Strategies for the Teaching of Reading

The training and development took three forms:

- readings on explicit teaching strategies,
- training and development sessions facilitated by our mentor in which we identified and talked about our own effective reading strategies in order for us to articulate these reading strategies to students in our classroom, and
- sharing practices we were trying in our classrooms as a result of our reading and training and development.

This, of course, involved discussion of successes, failures, and frustrations involved in our own attempts to come to terms with both new knowledge about reading and the methodology of explicit teaching. Tremendous energy was generated through these structured opportunities to explore our growing knowledge and observations. Each teacher was inspired to make connections with his or her own classroom practice. My concern as faculty leader was for us to share a common approach so that the effects would have a wider impact than on just the students in one class.

A reading that had significant impact on our team was John and Kate Munro's article, "Reading strategy teaching: A means of empowering those who find reading difficult" (1994. p. 9), in which students "are encouraged to take responsibility for their use of the strategies and to use them independently." Like many explicit approaches to the teaching of language, the teacher models the reading strategy. This approach differs from others, the authors argue, in that students identify the need to learn the strategy and are encouraged to talk about which strategies are useful and which are not. Ideally, once the students take more control over using the targeted strategy, they are able to apply it in a range of contexts. This suited our cross-curriculum approach to the teaching of reading in English and society and environment.

Another useful aspect of this approach was dividing reading strategies into before-reading strategies, during-reading strategies, and after-reading strategies. To assist student understanding, classroom documentation of reading strategies was divided into three sets and introduced to the students. Each was given a three-page handout with boxes to indicate the strategies used.

Reading Strategies to Help Become a Better Reader

A strategy is a way of doing something. If we want to improve how well we read, we need to think and talk about how we read now and what we can do to read better.

Before-Reading Strategies

These strategies help to prepare the mind for reading. Ask the following questions:

- Why are you reading? Are you reading for enjoyment or to get information? If you have to get information, what will you be expected to do with it? Answer comprehension questions? Summarize? Follow the instructions? Note the main points?

- What is the text about? Use titles, headings, subheadings, illustrations, or skim the first few pages to help find out what the text will be about.

- What do you know already about the topic? It helps to add new information to what is already known. It is like adding flesh to a skeleton. The skeleton is made up of all the bits of information you pull from memory. The flesh is the new information you get from reading.

- How will you go about reading? There are many ways to go about reading. Some may be more suitable than others:

    Will you listen to yourself read and make a picture of the information in your mind?

    Will you add to or change the picture that you have in mind?

    Will you try to work out the meaning of new words or guess and read on?

    Will you go back and reread sections that do not make sense?

During-Reading Strategies

These strategies will help you to understand what you are reading at the level of the word, the sentence, the section, and the whole text. Ask these questions:

- Where will you pause to think about what you have read? Try pausing at the end of a sentence, paragraph, or section to see which helps you to remember what you have read.

- When you come across a new word, will you guess and see what makes sense?

- Will you listen to yourself read in your mind as though you were reading aloud?

- Will you use punctuation to work out the meaning of a sentence?

- Will you form a picture in your mind from the information you have read? This picture can be changed with any new information found. If this strategy works, it sometimes helps to describe the picture to another person.

- Will you imagine yourself in the story or in the time that you are reading about? Ask yourself how you would feel, or what you would see or do.

- If you lose the meaning of what you are reading, will you go back and reread these parts?

- Will you ask questions while reading the text? What will happen next? What has this told me?

- Will you remind yourself why you are reading and how you are going about reading? This can help you stay on track when you lose concentration.

After-Reading Strategies

It may be tempting to skip strategies, but they are important to check how much you understood and remembered. They also help you think about which reading strategies helped you to read so that you can use them again or try other ones in other reading activities. Ask these questions:

- What did you learn or what was the story about?
- How well did the writer set out the information or story to help you understand?
- What reading strategies helped while you were reading?
- Did you learn anything new or unusual?
- Why did the writer write this material?
- How will you remember the information?

Try these remembering strategies:

- Describe the main ideas briefly.
- Connect the new information to what is already known.
- Draw a picture of the ideas.
- Draw a map of the ideas.
- Think about when these ideas could be used in the future.
- What new words were found in the text?
- When might you use these new words in the future?
- What words did I find hard to read?

(Adapted from Munro & Munro, 1994.)

More Reading Strategies

Another important aspect of the training and development was an introduction to the "four roles of a literate person" (Freebody & Luke, 1990), which are used in *Cornerstones* (see Preface, p. vi). This framework offers a window through which teachers can observe the readers in their classroom and helps students to understand the range of strategies employed by a successful reader. Within this framework a good reader will develop a range of reading strategies that can be employed to make sense of a text:

- As a *text decoder*, a good reader will employ a range of strategies to identify patterns in text at levels of letter, word, clause, or whole text.
- As a *text participant*, they will use prior knowledge in order to make personal and cognitive links with the text.
- As a *text user*, they will appreciate that different texts are required for different purposes.
- As a *text analyst*, they will be able to assess and, if necessary, challenge the world view of the text.

At times there was frustration as we attempted to synthesize the different ideas. A core group took on the challenge of assimilating the central ideas of before-, during-, and after-reading strategies and the four roles of a literate person into a manageable form.

One teacher documented the achievements in the four roles of a reader (see Figure 1 on pages 87–88), which she extracted from the reading strategy journals in both English and society and environment and, which helped to affirm a positive educational outcome. This list was useful in seeing how the reading strategies used in English were used in society and environment to help identify opportunities for teaching the strategies in each area.

An Observation Checklist

We created a checklist for monitoring students' reading strategies with fiction (see Figure 2 on pages 89–90), so we would know what to look for as we observed students in the four interdependent roles. The checklist provided a common framework and facilitated a more consistent approach among the teachers. The aim was to develop our own metacognition as well as the students' in these early learning stages. To help our own understanding, we identified the strategies involved in each reading role. A separate framework was developed for monitoring resource-based learning strategies.

How explicit must we be? was a frequently asked question and one we are still trying to answer. Any teacher or group of teachers who embark on this course will ultimately face the need to balance explicitness with classroom manageability.

Figure 1   Four Roles of a Reader

ENGLISH
Code Breaker
- Select the correct meaning of a homophone when reading a novel, e.g., in Theodore Taylor's *The Cay*, "There were no dykes here."
- Identify when different characters are speaking in texts where the author does not make this explicit.
- Determine how a change of setting or place of action is indicated in a novel.
- Use a variety of decoding strategies to make meaning of unfamiliar words.
- Decode the use of metaphors, symbols, and personification in a text.
- Employ strategies to clarify meaning in a text, e.g., reread the harder parts or read aloud.

Text Participant
- Relate events and characters and ideas in fictional texts with own knowledge and experience of the world.
- Use previous experiences with similar texts to facilitate reading.
- Identify with the concerns and dreams of particular characters in a fictional or biographical text.
- Read between the lines.

Text User
- Describe the ways in which fantasies, detective/crime, and science fiction are similar and different in their narrative structure.
- Recognize how the grammar of a text influences readability and impact.
- Appreciate how an author experiments with narrative features in order to tell his or her story, e.g., Gary Crew's *Strange Objects* or Robert Cormier's *I Am the Cheese*.
- Identify features of style, e.g., narrative point of view, narrative sequence, irony, etc.

Text Analyst
- Recognize that no text is neutral.
- Identify the ways in which information or ideas are expressed and influence reader perceptions.
- Recognize and challenge how a writer positions a reader to view the world of the text or certain characters' action in a particular way.

SOCIETY and ENVIRONMENT
Code Breaker
- Identify the difference between unfamiliar names and subject-specific words, e.g., *Tutankhamen* and *shadoof*.
- Unpack meaning from a complex sentence such as one found in an encyclopedia.
- Recognize the hierarchy of information indicated by headings, subheadings, and highlighted keywords.

continued

Figure I   Four Roles of a Reader (continued)

- Recognize the use of connective words (*consequently, similarly, on the other hand*) and reference items (*it, them, her*).
- Give coherence of ideas to a text.
- Use a glossary to understand key words.
- Employ strategies to clarify meaning in a text, e.g., reread the harder parts.

Text Participant

- Draw on background knowledge of the topic in order to build further knowledge through research.
- Use noting schemata such as idea maps or structured overviews to direct reading.
- Recognize that reading on a subject is more depersonalized than English.
- Identify and reconcile discrepancies among existing knowledge and new information or information drawn from different sources.
- Develop a visual impression of what is being read and add detail to the mental picture as the information base widens.

Text User

- Recognize that each text type has different linguistic structures and features, which can facilitate reading, e.g., diaries and journals, interview transcripts, oral histories, reports, graphs, and secondary sources of information such as reference books.
- Identify how important information in a sentence or clause is thematized by placing it at the front.
- Recognize and explain how encyclopedia entries are structured at a whole-text level.
- Assess the appropriateness of different sources of information for different research tasks.

Text Analyst

- Recognize that no text is neutral.
- Recognize levels of objectivity and subjectivity in both primary and secondary sources of information.
- Identify how different authors portray the same event in different ways and explain their reasons for advancing these different perspectives.
- Identify the ways in which information or ideas are expressed and influence reader perceptions.

Adapted from *Cornerstones*, Module 4 (1995) and Freebody & Luke (1990).

FIGURE 2   Observation Checklist

NAME: _____

TEACHER: _____

DATE: _____

Four Roles of a Literate Person
CB = Code Breaker
TP = Text Participant
TU = Text User
TA = Text Analyst

Before Reading/Preparing to read

Knowledge of the text type

What is the book called? (CB)
What is the name of the author? (CB)
What kind of book do you think it will be? (TU)
Who do you think the book was written for? Why? (TA)

Beginning stage	Early achievement		Growth	Extension
I_____	I_____		I_____	I

Predicting the story before reading

What clues about the story can we find on the book? (CB)
What might the story be about? (TP)
What do you already know about the topic? (TP)

Beginning stage	Early achievement		Growth	Extension
I_____	I_____		I_____	I

During Reading/Making meaning of the text

	Beginning	Early	Growth	Extension
Pronounces words clearly (CB)	I_____	I_____	I_____	I
Uses clues in the meaning of a sentence to work out a new word (CB)	I_____	I_____	I_____	I
Uses rules of grammar to work out a new word (CB)	I_____	I_____	I_____	I

continued

FIGURE 2   Observation Checklist (continued)

| Can use letter knowledge of letter blends or word derivations to attack a new word (CB) | Beginning I_____ Early I_____ Growth I_____ Extension I |

Can use letter knowledge of letter
blends or word derivations
to attack a new word (CB)　　　Beginning　Early　Growth　Extension
　　　　　　　　　　　　　　I_____I_____I_____I

Self-corrects to make meaning
clearer (TP)　　　　　　　　　Beginning　Early　Growth　Extension
　　　　　　　　　　　　　　I_____I_____I_____I

Expression in voice shows
clearer (TP)　　　　　　　　　Beginning　Early　Growth　Extension
　　　　　　　　　　　　　　I_____I_____I_____I

Uses punctuation cues to
work out meaning (CB)　　　　　Beginning　Early　Growth　Extension
　　　　　　　　　　　　　　I_____I_____I_____I

Uses evidence in the story and
knowledge of the kind of book
to predict the ending (TP)　　　Beginning　Early　Growth　Extension
　　　　　　　　　　　　　　I_____I_____I_____I

During and After Reading/Understanding of the text

Discussion or reading journal shows the following aspects of comprehension, appreciation, and analysis:

Can link events and characters
to own experience and background
knowledge (TP)　　　　　　　Beginning　Early　Growth　Extension
　　　　　　　　　　　　　　I_____I_____I_____I

Can link the story to other texts (TP)　Beginning　Early　Growth　Extension
　　　　　　　　　　　　　　I_____I_____I_____I

Can form a mental picture from the
words in a text (TP)　　　　　　Beginning　Early　Growth　Extension
　　　　　　　　　　　　　　I_____I_____I_____I

Can retell information about the plot
character and message (TP)　　　Beginning　Early　Growth　Extension
　　　　　　　　　　　　　　I_____I_____I_____I

Has an opinion about events and
characters in the text and uses
information from the text to
support opinions (TA)　　　　　Beginning　Early　Growth　Extension
　　　　　　　　　　　　　　I_____I_____I_____I

Can explain what the writer wanted
to get across to the reader by writing
the book (TA)　　　　　　　　Beginning　Early　Growth　Extension
　　　　　　　　　　　　　　I_____I_____I_____I

Can see what the writer does to
influence the opinions of the reader
(TA)　　　　　　　　　　　　Beginning　Early　Growth　Extension
　　　　　　　　　　　　　　I_____I_____I_____I

The Role of Reading Strategy Journals

One of the concerns expressed by researchers is whether explicit teaching really connects with students' understanding. Freebody, Ludwig, and Gunn (1995), in their study of literacy practices in and out of school, describe numerous instances in which their classroom observations and analyses of teacher-student talk indicated that often "the students do not cue into the perspective represented in the teacher's talk" (p. 297). The teacher's aim may be metacognition, but they need to ensure that students are engaged adequately with the ideas and reading strategies in order for metacognition to take place. The study outlines a range of "interactive trouble" (see Preface, p. vii), which can impede students' understanding of what teachers want them to know.

The study identifies causes such as *epistemological trouble*, when the teacher mis-reads the student feedback and thinks they understand when, in fact, they do not; *organizational trouble*, when student responses do not fit the established classroom routines; and *stylistic trouble*, when the students' preferred way of expressing their understanding is not preferred by the teacher. The implications for students from social, cultural, and economic backgrounds that are different from the teacher are clear: Teachers must monitor students' understandings and make explicit those understandings that they have previously assumed students will grasp.

So how could we be more inclusive in monitoring students' level of metacognition and then improve our effectiveness in explicating the reading strategies, which we would like students to practice, think, and adopt or reject? A reading strategy journal was the method of monitoring students' understanding, which two teachers adopted. In two of four classes, the teachers used a reading strategy journal in both English and in society and environment to encourage students to articulate what they understood and which reading strategies had been taught.

There were additional factors in our decision to try the use of reading strategy journals. First, we found a number of problems with having teacher observations as the single source of student achievement data. With classes of 30, it was difficult to find the required time to observe students in a range of reading tasks. Second, concentrated observation can often be interrupted. Third, a teacher often privileges particular ways that students communicate reading strategies they are attempting—particularly under the pressure of time in secondary schools. This can disadvantage students from backgrounds that differ from the teacher's. For example, students from non–English-speaking backgrounds may feel daunted if they have to demonstrate their knowledge in group discussions.

As teachers, we must allow ourselves time to be inclusive in our assessment practices. Well-managed, reading-strategy journals have allowed teachers time away from the classroom to contemplate and assess the students' ability to articulate and use particular reading strategies.

So what can teachers learn from the reading journal? This depends on what questions the teacher asks to guide student reflection and writing. If students regard the journal as a place to regurgitate facts, the teacher will learn little more than what they would through tests or projects. This is why we increasingly refined the kinds of questions students were asked to consider in their journals. We asked them to consider and record the strategies they used before, during, and after reading, as well as the strategies they had difficulty with. The handout of strategies was a useful reference for students as they wrote in their journals.

Both teachers who tried the use of reading journals in society and environment found that students initially wanted to write about content only. They found strategy learning to be a more difficult concept for students. In order to overcome this, it was necessary to model once again insightful responses. This was done by teachers modeling responses about strategies and sharing the responses of students who were more able to articulate the reading strategies they had employed. By sharing student responses on overhead transparencies, teachers found that the level of reflection improved among the whole class.

A few excerpts from students' reading strategy journals in both society and environment and English demonstrated the students' attempts to articulate the reading strategies introduced in class. The following comments show that they were clear about what textual features either supported or frustrated their comprehension:

The reference books have got clear contents and an index. The headings and subheadings are clear. There are no glossarys (sic) to help me understand important words. Key words were not highlighted.

The information that the book gave was different to the subheading. It got very annoying. I still have no idea on how to set up my research. It's difficult to choose where I'm going to put my information; under what subheadings?

The sentences in this book didn't have lots of ideas in them. They were spaced out so that people could understand them.

I haven't heard the word *shikkered* before. Must find out what it means. I really think that if some racist people read this book they would enjoy it and change their mind about black people.

Other students used wording from the handout about reading strategies to scaffold their own attempts to articulate the strategies they were employing:

The strategies helping me are, "Will I pause for a short time to think about what I read?" and "If I start to loose (sic) the meaning of a word, I will go back and look at it."

The reading strategy journals helped teachers to identify areas in which to focus work with individual students; for example:

I still have a bit of difficulty finding and translating words into more easier and more meaning full (sic) words.

The following comment by a Negotiated Curriculum Plan[2] (NCP) student is most rewarding because it shows the student making conscious choices about which pre-reading strategies are most useful:

I think you have ideas maps because you can get all the big headings and put little ones onto them. But the guiding questions are better. They help me more.

In the English reading journals, students operated as text participants, making connections with their world:

When you read this book, you can see pictures in your head of everything. That's how well the author describes it .... It is good that the author told me where this is all happening, unlike the last book I read. It's also about asbestos which is a bit of a coincidence. (We had been writing letters on asbestos issues to the editor of the local press in the Port Adelaide, SA, area.)

The world in which they live is very like our own. The book faces the reader with real-life issues such as contracting a virus and losing the people we love. The characters at Kim's school are very ignorant towards the issue of AIDS, and I think that is how people in our world would act if that happened to someone.

The students were still in the early stages of exploring and articulating a range of reading strategies, but the results looked promising.

Teacher Response to the Explicit Teaching of Reading Project

Throughout the project, we made a priority of allowing time away from classroom responsibilities to share experiences and reflect on progress. At a debriefing session, the teacher responses indicated the level of enthusiasm for opportunities in classroom research:

As a school we gained through opening up the whole dialogue about reading and reading difficulties. The project itself showed how important reading skills are. Students perceived that we were working toward improving their skills, which was evident in how often they asked questions about their reading and examined their own reading strategies.

(Karen O'Neill, English and special education teacher, offered classroom support and worked with NCP students.)

Through the use of reading journals in both English and society and environment, students began to verbalize the texts they found difficult and, more importantly, what they could do when challenged by these texts. They were given a shared language to talk about the processes of reading. (Jenny Switala, Year 8 society and environment and English teacher)

The project gave us a language to talk about reading. When teachers are explicit about the range of strategies that good readers use, the students can acknowledge what they do well and experiment with new strategies. We developed a wide range of strategies that could be selected. Having a shared language to talk about reading is vital to teachers. Ideas and resources can be more effectively shared. (Meredith Edwards, project coordinator, English coordinator, and Year 8 coordinator.)

We worked on improving students' metacognitive skills to improve their perception of how they read and how they could improve their own reading. This, I believe, made them more comfortable as learners. I also think that there have been great benefits for our NCP students. Reading is an area in which they struggle, and I think giving them clear guidelines on how to approach reading is helpful. Opening the dialogue probably improved their perception of themselves as learners. They see themselves as learners—in the same boat as everyone else. (Karen O'Neill)

My involvement in the project with other Year 8 teachers being explicit about teaching reading has been fantastic. I constantly compare it to art, which is my main teaching area. I knew the strategies, but making them explicit helps me to put them in clear categories and sequence. I'm continually amazed how areas in secondary schools continue to work in isolation; at least in middle school, we are aware of how transferrable these skills are across the subjects. The project also made us look at our own knowledge base and teaching skills in this area. (Cushla O'Sullivan, art teacher; offered literacy support in two classes.)

Much of what English teachers should know about their students in order to attribute reading (and viewing) outcomes is learned by observing students in society and environment. (Meredith Edwards)

The responses led to the following insights about our professional development and about explicit teaching:

1. We recognized that the collaborative project was raising students' and teachers' awareness and appreciation of specific reading strategies.

2. The project introduced a shared language for students and teachers, which helped in making explicit the specific reading strategies.

3. Explicit teaching could increase students' control over their learning and confidence in their learning.

4. Explicit teaching prompted teachers to articulate specific learning goals for particular students. This gave teachers insight into their students as readers and enabled them to set specific goals to work on with individual students. (Jenny Switala)

5. The advantages observed in English and society and environment are applicable to other learning areas.

6. We were able to see the value of working across curriculum.

From a coordinator's point of view, the project supported a team of teachers to pursue their own concerns within a shared classroom research project. Involvement in the explicit teaching of reading project has provided an invaluable opportunity for professional renewal and team building among a group of Year 8 teachers. The enthusiasm generated by individuals, who were able to pursue their own areas of classroom research within our shared project aims, was infectious. It inspired each of us not only to go further in our own research tasks, but also to synthesize the ideas of other team members into our own evolving practices within this area of teaching.

In Conclusion

It is clear from the comments that the teachers involved in the project gained significantly from working together on the explicit teaching of reading. Exploring a range of strategies, discussing successes and concerns, and sharing frameworks developed for use with the students contributed to a common understanding. This shared understanding meant that we had a common language to use with the students, a set of strategies that we felt confident about in our teaching, and a framework that we could introduce to students and reinforce in one class to the next.

These common understandings provide a strong foundation on which to make judgments about student achievement, and to plan for improvements in teaching and articulating further reading strategies. We identified a productive way of developing our confidence and effectiveness as teachers in cooperation with colleagues who teach other subjects or who have specialist responsibilities in supporting students.

As coordinator of English and literacy, I will look for other projects that will provide support and input to help us develop other aspects of our teaching, which the curriculum now requires of us.

References

Cornerstones: Training and development program. (Module 5). (1995). Adelaide, SA: Department of Education and Children's Services, Curriculum Division.

Curriculum Corporation. (1994). *English—A curriculum profile for Australian schools.* Carlton, VIC: Author.

Freebody, P., Ludwig, C., & Gunn, S. (1995). Everyday literacy practices in and out of school. In *Children's Literacy National Project* (Vol. 1, pp. 297–315). Adelaide, SA: Department of Education, Employment, and Training.

Freebody, P., & Luke, A. (1990). Literacies' programs: Debates and demands in cultural contexts. *Prospect: Journal of Adult Migrant Education Programs, 5*(3), 7–16.

Munro, J., & Munro, K. (1994). Reading strategy teaching: A means of empowering those who find reading difficult. *The Australian Journal of Language and Literacy, 17*(1), 7–23.

Wilkinson, L. (1995). Explicit teaching. In *Cornerstones: Training and development program* (Module 6 & 7, Appendix 1). Adelaide, SA: Department of Education and Children's Services, Curriculum Division.

Notes

[1] In most Australian states, teachers are required to assign achievement levels in eight areas of learning, of which English is one. In assigning levels, teachers in South Australia use the nationally developed *English—A curriculum profile for Australian schools* (1994), which describes a progression of achievement from Year 1 to the end of secondary school in three strands: Writing, Speaking and listening, and Reading and viewing.

[2] The Negotiated Curriculum Plan in South Australia identifies those students who are in need of an individualized learning and teaching program.

Chapter Eight

Explicitly Teaching the Reading of Nonfiction Texts

Jay Marshall

As the learning support coordinator at an independent college in South Australia, Jay Marshall devised a program for supporting students deemed at risk because of their limited literacy skills. She also works with teachers to help all students, not just those at risk, to develop literacy strategies that will bring them success as readers and writers.

For her classroom research, Jay worked with another teacher to explicitly teach reading strategies for nonfiction texts, and to ascertain how useful the students found these strategies. She made the strategies explicit to the students by having them brainstorm their current strategies and reflect on the value of those strategies, and by explaining, demonstrating, and providing practice in using specific strategies.

As learning support coordinator, I introduced strategies for essay writing to middle school students and teachers. (At Woodcroft College, middle school includes Years 6 to 10.) The students appeared to find these strategies useful, but I had doubts. Were students finding these strategies useful? Did the students understand why they were using these strategies? Did the strategies improve learning outcomes for all the students?

To find answers to these questions, I worked with Rebecca Clark, a middle school humanities teacher, and one of her Year 8 classes, which represented a broad range of abilities. I found the class energetic and vocal about what was presented to them, which was ideal for asking them about the strategies being taught.

Rebecca and I developed a unit on ancient Greece, incorporating the reading strategies we wanted to teach and assess. We planned to teach the strategies as part of the unit, and to ask the students for their views at the beginning, middle, and end.

The unit was divided into the following stages:

- Ask students, using a questionnaire, how they plan for and feel about writing essays.
- Explicitly teach what makes a good reader.
- Introduce the topic with a concept map.
- Teach extracting notes from a text.
- Teach the use of headings, subheadings, topic sentences, and illustrations for obtaining information.
- Teach building notes into a framework.
- Ask students how valuable they thought the strategies were so far by distributing a questionnaire.
- Explicitly teach the features of a travel brochure.
- Introduce the assessment criteria.
- Assess the approach by having students write letters to the teachers about their views and how useful they found the unit.

One way to help students become independent learners is to make them aware of the strategies they use and value. I realized that the questionnaires and letters accomplished this and informed us.

Step 1: Ask the Students

The students completed a clearly outlined questionnaire in which they were asked to reveal their feelings about reading, finding books, and taking notes when researching for essays and assignments. The following questions were asked:

1. You have been asked to write a history essay.
   How do you feel?   Oh no!   OK   I quite like writing essays.
2. How often do you plan an essay *before* you write or read for information?
   Never   Sometimes   Always
3. How do you feel about writing an introduction?
   Not confident   OK   No problem
   A topic sentence?
   What's that?   I have some idea.   No problem

I wondered if I could have been more explicit about what sort of essay?

From the questionnaire, we discovered that 25% of girls and 4% of boys answered "Oh no!" when asked to write an essay, and only 1 student out of 23 quite liked and felt confident about writing essays. The difference between the responses of boys and girls was of particular interest: Boys were twice as likely to dislike writing essays as girls. How could this dislike be addressed in our teaching?

In addition, 17% of students never planned essays and 17%always planned essays, which left 66%who sometimes planned essays. Sixty-three percent of students had some idea about introductions and topic sentences, while 15% were not confident about introductions and topic sentences, and 21% were confident. We concluded that Rebecca's teaching approach meant some students grew confident with their writing skills, but some, particularly boys, still lacked confidence and skills.

Although the information was useful, the main aim of the questionnaire was for students to explore how they were doing with reading, researching, and writing essays and assignments. We wanted students to think about what they did well and what they would like to improve. If they wanted to become better readers, they would be receptive to the reading strategies that would be introduced during the unit on ancient Greece. We wanted students to see the relevance of strategies we were using already with the group. This aim was made clear to the students.

As a first-time teacher-researcher, I questioned whether the information I was gathering would have relevance for other teachers.

Step 2: What Makes a Good Reader?

The class and I brainstormed about what makes a good reader. Students identified strategies they could use to develop reading skills, which would support those who had a limited repertoire of strategies or had not been able to develop strategies to assist their reading. Strategies were listed on a chart, placed in a prominent position in the classroom, and copied into exercise books. The language and sequence of points were the students'.

- Reading aloud helps you read fluently.
- Concentrate on what you read—don't get distracted.
- Understand what you read.
- Be a good speller.
- Enjoy what you're reading.
- Find it easy to choose books.
- Read every word carefully, but skim and scan if needed.
- Know why you are reading.
- Know what the words mean.
- Be committed to your reading.

- Read regularly.
- Practice.
- Read at a reasonable rate.
- Choose the right book.
- Know how to read a new word:
     break it down into pieces, i.e., syllables
     recognize sounds
     read around the word to try and work out what it means.
- Ask questions.

I have since created lists with students on strategies for being a good speller and a good writer, which is an excellent way to develop and share useful strategies.

Step 3: Explicitly Introduce the Topic

Students were introduced to the topic Ancient Greece and to the end product, which would be a travel brochure. They were asked to share what they already knew about ancient Greece. We had thought most would have had some prior knowledge, but few had.

We collected all prior knowledge of ancient Greece on a concept map (see Figure 1) and explained that main idea circles were reading signposts and the words added were street signs. Recognizing these words as they read would support their reading.

FIGURE 1   Concept Map on Ancient Greece

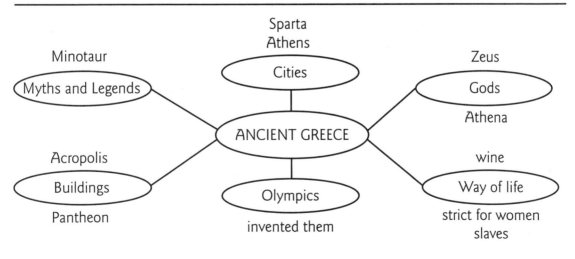

The main topic was written in the center of the map and was broken down into subtopics, which were placed in one idea circle. The teacher guided students as to what constitutes a subtopic.

Example street-sign words were added by the teacher around the related idea circles to model the approach. Groups of students discussed extra words that were added around each idea circle. These words were shared, and the teacher added extra street signs and idea circles.

Step 4: Teach Note Taking

Students were directed to a chapter on ancient Greece in their textbook *Ancient World* (Sawyer, 1990), which was divided into six main topics: myths and legends, Athens, Sparta, battles, Alexander the Great, and ancient Olympics.

The students formed groups of six, and each student in the group took notes on one of the six topics. They then shared their notes within their group, which provided an overview of the whole chapter before starting more detailed work on each subtopic. (This activity is appropriate whenever a text can be divided into discrete sections.)

FIGURE 2   Sticky Note

ATHENS
– ancient & modern capital of Greece
– first democratic government
– built around Acropolis
– cultural center, ancient Greece
– important C5th BC city
– rival city to Sparta
– noted for philosophy & drama
– Ancient Athens - 20,000 people

Each student had a sticky note on which to write notes (see Figure 2). They were told to write on their sticky notes 10 interesting facts from their allotted section of the chapter. Students began by reading the topic sentence of each paragraph.

On the chalkboard and referring to the textbook, we modeled how a note might be extracted from the text and how it might be worded.

In retrospect, I realized we could have been more explicit about what constitutes a note.

Step 5: Teach Using Headings, Subheadings, Topic Sentences, and Illustrations When Taking Notes

The students were introduced to the strategy of using headings, subheadings, topic sentences, and illustrations as a strategy for contending with the daunting quantity of reading in the middle school. Working on the subtopic, Athens, the students were told to

- read first the headings and subheadings and record anything they learned from these words,
- look at illustrations and record any learned information,
- read the topic sentences of each paragraph.

Students often found they needed to read no further. They recorded the information on a framework (see Step 6).

This is a valuable strategy for reading nonfiction texts. Students learned to write a well-constructed paragraph as it became apparent that paragraphs needed topic sentences and that paragraphs must elaborate on that topic. Information not relating to the topic sentence was not to be included. When topic sentences did not inform students about the content of the paragraph, they soon said so. They became critical readers of text.

Reading topic sentences is best taught by highlighting the topic sentences of a text on an overhead transparency.

I initially wondered whether having students read the topic sentence and nothing more would deny them the depth of information offered in the text. However, I feel this strategy gets students through what might otherwise appear an overwhelming amount of reading. The more confident readers could read further.

Step 6: Teach How to Build Notes Into a Framework

We introduced a framework for collating the notes (see Figure 3 on page 103) from each of the six sections in the chapter on ancient Greece. We explained that by completing this framework the students would have an overview of the whole chapter, and they could use the summary notes to help them complete more detailed work on each section.

The framework supported the students' reading by providing a guide to the chapter and by introducing key vocabulary words. This strategy is particularly valuable because it shares the reading load across the group.

A framework consists of six boxes in which notes are recorded under the subtopic headings. Subtopics can be written in by the teacher to guide students' reading. The wording of the subtopics (at the top of each box) will appear in the topic sentence of each paragraph of the essay or assignment. Each box is generally a paragraph.

When each student completed the sticky note, the groups reconvened and each group member shared his or her notes to complete the framework. As each student read his or her notes, the other students filled in the relevant section of their framework. For example, one student shared notes on myths and legends, and another shared notes on Sparta.

FIGURE 3   Framework for Notes

Myths and legends	Athens	Sparta
• • •		
Battles	Alexander the Great	Ancient Olympics

The teachers and I often questioned why six should be the set number of boxes in a framework, but we found that six boxes meet most requirements.

The Halfway Stage

Students had had the opportunity to look at themselves as readers within the humanities classroom in the introductory questionnaire; to explicitly explore the skills required to be a good reader; and to have explained explicitly reading strategies, which they could use as they completed their unit on ancient Greece. These reading strategies were

- recording prior knowledge on a concept map,
- sharing reading within a group,

- using a sticky note for note taking,
- using a framework to provide order to notes and an overview of the topic, and
- using headings, subheadings, illustrations, and topic sentences to see the text structure.

I summarized progress made to date by talking to the students, which I do all the time now.

What point have we reached?

What have we achieved?

Step 7: The Halfway-Stage Questionnaire

A questionnaire was designed to check progress and was completed with me reading and explaining each question. The students recorded their answers. In this way, no student was disadvantaged if they found the questions difficult. The results of the questionnaire are detailed in Tables 1 and 2.

I made clear that honest answers were required. We did not want students writing answers they thought we wanted or telling us they found something useful when they did not. We explained that we wanted to know if the strategies we were teaching were helping. And if they said they liked the strategies, we would be teaching them this way for the rest of the year. This was their opportunity to say how they wanted topics to be taught and if ideas were needed to support their reading.

Table 1 shows that a majority found all but the sticky notes valuable. Table 2 reveals that boys were more enthusiastic about the strategies than girls. When we talked to the group, the girls who had not responded positively to the strategies said it was not that these strategies were confusing, but that they already had strategies they used

TABLE I   Percentage of Students Finding Strategies Useful

STRATEGY	% finding this strategy useful
Using information maps	68% found maps useful for recording
Reading topic sentences first	75% found this strategy helped reading
Framework	68% found this made recording information clearer
Sharing reading load by sharing notes	75% felt they learned a lot working in this way
Sticky notes	54% of students found this helpful

TABLE 2   Gender Differences in Finding Strategies Useful

RESPONSES (*N* = 28)	Boys	Girls
Found topic sentences useful when reading	89%	50%
Found framework useful when making notes	72%	60%
Found using sticky notes useful for note taking	61%	44%
Found work easier than normal by using this explicit approach	72%	60%

when reading. The students who were most enthusiastic about the strategies were those who often experienced difficulties when reading. The conclusion we drew was that students who were already experiencing success continued to approach work as they had in the past, while students who had experienced difficulties now had strategies they could use when reading, note taking, and preparing for written responses.

I realized that boys appreciated being taught structured strategies, but how did the girls already know the strategies?

Step 8: Explicitly Teach the Features of a Travel Brochure

The students' final task was to put together a travel brochure about traveling back in time to ancient Greece. At the halfway stage, 27 out of 28 students were clear about the result of this unit, because the final task was referred to when we introduced each session. The work they were doing provided information to create a brochure about ancient Greece.

The students brought in brochures to consider how they were constructed and the language used. The key features and components of a travel brochure were brainstormed, written on a map, and recorded in books. Using the list of features, Rebecca designed a proforma layout of the brochure. The students regarded the proforma as very supportive.

Students responded well to fill-in boxes or a proforma to follow, which made the task clear. Students were confident about what was expected of them.

Step 9: Introduce the Assessment Criteria

Before beginning the task, the class had negotiated six assessment criteria for their work. The group discussed what they would need to be successful in creating a travel brochure. Suggestions were recorded on the chalkboard and summarized into six criteria for success. The assessment criteria were explicit to the students, which they had negotiated as a group:

1. Travel brochure is neat and attractively presented.
2. All six areas of study are included in the brochure.
3. At least three facts are included in each section.
4. Appropriate spelling, grammar, and punctuation has been used.
5. Effort has been put into the gathering of pictures and ideas for the brochure.
6. There is evidence of thorough planning and drafting.

The completed brochures were well done and attractive (see Figure 4). They showed thought and were laid out clearly. There were some gifted students in the class, and one student with a mild learning disability. This student's work was not distinguishable from the rest; he had produced an outstanding piece of work. In his questionnaire and letter, he responded positively to this explicit approach to reading strategies.

Step 10: Assessing the Approach by Asking Students

The students wrote letters to Rebecca and me about how they felt about their work on ancient Greece.

Rebecca brainstormed with the group the strategies used and why the students used each strategy. As with the questionnaire, honest answers were stressed. Some of their responses were as follows:

> I liked Ancient Greece because you gave us lots of information so that we knew what we were doing.

> The topic sentences (were good) because then you have a good idea about what the paragraph is about and that helps you find information.

ᴀNCIᴇNᴛ GᴙᴇᴇCᴇ

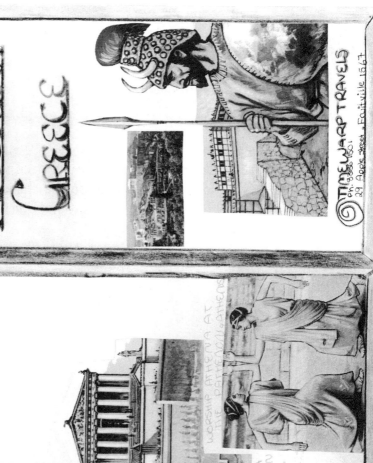

© TIMEWARP TRAVELS
Ph. 9356 1501
29 Apple Street, Eastville 1567

continued

Attractions

There's heaps to do in Greece like shopping, worshipping, dancing, site seeing & debating. If you have any specific things you wish to do, we can arrange a tour for you. Call us on 9356 1501.

The manager of
Timewarp Travels
R.A. Rawson.

WORSHIP ATHENA AT THE PARTHENON, ATHENS.

WATCH A DANCE IN SPARTA.

Accommodations

★ The Athens Inn
1 Adult = 3 gold coins per night.
1 Child = 1 gold & 3 silver coins per night. Your stay includes all 3 meals.

★ The Athena Inn
1 Adult = luxery = 6 gold coins per night.
= average = 3 gold coins per night.
1 child = luxery = 3 gold coins per night
= average = 1 gold coin per night
This deal includes all meals & breakfast in bed.

The Athena Inn

★ The Spartan Berry
1 person = 1 gold & 1 bronze coins.
This package offers a bedroom & personal washroom. No meal included.

FIGURE 4 Student's Completed Travel Brochure (continued)

INTRODUCTION!!!!

Visit the most beautiful & artistic country of them all, GREECE, with Timewarp Travels.

As a time traveller you'll experience a new & exciting culture with many Gods & Myths.

When you arrive in Greece you will notice the dramatic landscape - snowy mountains, shady valleys & deep gorges. This beauty is like nothing else in the world.

Greece is very famous for its statues & theatre & you won't be disappointed. With many screenings of plays a week you're sure not to miss one. Also their artwork is on display all over the romantic country so keep an eye out for it.

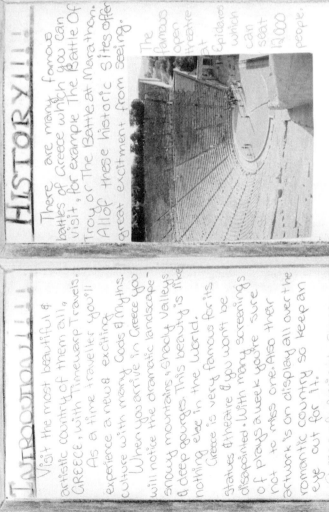

GREECE : ANCIENT GREECE

HISTORY!!!!

There are many famous battles of Greece which you can visit, for example The Battle Of Troy or The Battle at Marathon. All of these historic sites offer great excitment from seeing.

The famous open theatre at Epidaros which can seat 12,000 people.

Or maybe the Olympics & Mount Olympus are your cup of tea. Either way you can book your tickets both, of these & other interesting sites of Myths & legends.

Because you'll have plenty of money to shop around with why not take a trip to Athens & the markets there. Or maybe you could vote on the Ostraka or worship Athena at the Parthenon.

LIFESTYLE!!!!

An Ancient Greek town.

Greeks were very superstitious & often prayed & gave sacrifices to the Gods. They did this to prepare themselves for disease, shipwrecks, war & childbirth. As these disasters can strike anytime in the harsh but beautiful country of Greece.

Greek women were not often seen in public, unless they gave a performance. This is because they have to run a house hold & mainly entertained at home.

When you arrive in Greece you'll find people get around in horse & cart those back or walk. Even though their not that advanced the carts are very luxurious.

Greek clothing is very comfortable. Men wore togas. Women wore a single piece of material with many folds to create a a piece outfit effect.

I thought my end result was pretty good compared to when I had to do assignments without a concept map and example.

I didn't like (sharing information) because sometimes you don't get a very good group and they always muck around.

I think that reading the topic sentences is much easier and quicker, however sometimes you don't get the total amount of information needed.

As well as informing us, the students' reflections on the value of strategies they used helped them become independent learners.

The task sheet (see Figure 5) for use in future units was not used with this particular class. It includes all stages of the program we followed, some of which were not discussed here. The response approaches commonly used in classrooms need no explanation: diary entries, posters, and quizzes.

What Did We as Teachers Learn About Being Explicit?

After this unit, Rebecca and I felt more confident about working with the strategies we had devised to support the reading of nonfiction texts. We suggested they be used by other staff in their classrooms. We felt we had been explicit and clear with the students about what we were doing and why we engaged them in the learning process. The idea of planning a unit thoroughly before teaching begins and making students clear about the end goal was confirmed. Laying out a path to follow supports both teachers and students.

Where to From Here?

Not everything went smoothly. Student responses revealed that few felt confident about note taking. Although reading topic sentences and using the six-box framework were useful, some students were not sure about what constitutes a note, a keyword, or a point. They were able to find and classify information they wanted using the framework, but found it difficult to write notes without writing whole sentences. So, we devised explicit strategies to look at note taking:

- crossing out all unnecessary words in a text and writing up remaining words in a new text,
- modeling the note-taking process on an overhead transparency, and
- encouraging the use of highlighters to extract key words.

The work Rebecca and I did with the group showed the importance of clear and explicit support. We realized that a task sheet provided at the start of a unit gave stu-

FIGURE 5   Explicit Task Sheet

Topic:	Ancient Greece
Task:	Travel Brochure to Ancient Greece
Due date:	Thursday 3rd July; Week 10, Term 2

Task Completed (Tick as you complete)	Tick	Date
1 Complete a class concept map on Ancient Greece		
2 Fill in six box headings on framework		
3 Complete sticky note on section given to you by teacher from text book on Ancient Greece—note taking		
4 Copy your notes into correct framework box		
5 Share your notes with your group		
6 Complete your framework by listening to each group member's notes		
7 Myths and Legends—find your own myth		
8 Sparta—listen to description of life in Sparta and write diary entry of Spartan		
9 Complete a cloze exercise on Sparta		
10 Athens—take notes using topic sentences only		
11 Olympic Games—complete group concept map		
12 Make poster advertising Ancient games		
13 Battles—group quiz, skim for answers, time limit		
14 Bring in examples of travel brochures		
15 Brainstorm together about brochure contents		
16 Negotiate class criteria to meet when completing travel brochure		
17 Look at brochure outline from teacher		
18 Library session—any extra research		
19 Write a rough draft using your notes		
20 Check work using a checklist		
21 Get a friend to check work		
22 Write a neat copy		

dents a helpful overview to show where each step and strategy was leading. The sequencing and breakdown of tasks proved useful with classes in the middle and senior schools and adopted in other teaching areas.

Explicit teaching is now the core of Rebecca's and my teaching. In 1998, I wrote *The Inclusive Teaching Strategies Book* that includes input from teachers in all curriculum areas. The explicit approach is finding its place in our school's everyday teaching.

The most valuable part of completing this classroom research was working with teachers who focused on teaching reading explicitly, and who worked with students at different grade levels. This was my first experience with action research, and it will not be my last.

References

Marshall, J. (Ed.). (1998). *The inclusive teaching strategies book*. Adelaide, SA: Woodcroft College.
Sawyer, R. (1990). *Ancient world*. Marrickville, NSW: Science Press.

Chapter Nine

But What Do We Make Explicit?

Betty Weeks

As a project officer for early literacy in the South Australian Education Department, Betty Weeks developed a workshop for teachers to help them see how explicit teaching could be a part of every aspect of their early literacy program. Here she outlines a unit of work highlighting the ways in which teachers can make clear to students the different literacy skills and the value of the processes they were using. The unit of work includes planning for research, finding information, note taking, sharing information gathered, and writing and presenting a report. Teaching strategies used most for making these processes explicit are demonstrating them, thinking aloud the choices being made, and discussing the skills used with students.

xplicit teaching is a term that has recently generated a great deal of interest in educational circles. In my mind, it resonates with the words of Lisa Delpit (1988), who challenged educators to stop assuming that if we immersed children in language they would simply pick up the skills in a natural and easy manner.

Delpit demonstrates that in mainstream classrooms teachers often have operated according to unstated rules, which students have been expected to understand implicitly. She identifies "cultures of power" whereby teachers and successful participants appear to understand the rules, while those outside of that culture did not. An example is the use of indirect verbal directives such as "Would you mind closing the door?" instead of the more direct "Please close the door." Delpit argues that classrooms are replete with this kind of indirect instruction, particularly in relation to literacy, and that this is particularly confusing for those minority groups whose home cultures favor a more direct or explicit kind of instruction.

Delpit's powerful arguments have influenced many teachers to reevaluate their teaching practices and to identify aspects of literacy that they need to make more explicit in order for their students to be successful. Some of these outcomes are easy to identify because they are the conventions or basic skills such as correct spelling and grammar. Others are less easily observed and comprise those invisible aspects of literacy that teachers might assume students have acquired through familiarity and immersion in literacy activities at home and, which closely resemble those used in schools. Examples of these skills include the complex range of processes that occur in the reader's head when reading a passage of text or the monitoring and self-correction processes in which writers engage when composing.

Teachers can explicitly teach these skills by

- demonstrating them,
- thinking aloud to make the mental processes evident,
- involving students in activities that guide them to develop and practice the skills,
- talking about or discussing the skills, or
- combining all these strategies.

The "Talking Drawings" Unit

The Early Years Literacy Team in South Australia is frequently asked to provide workshop sessions for teachers to help them use explicit teaching methods. One strategy we have used successfully was adapted from an article by Suzanne McConnell (1992), in which she describes a strategy called "talking drawings" as a basis for exploring understandings and assisting learning in an adult literacy class.

The process we used was to select a topic related to one or more curriculum study areas and to take participants through a series of connected activities—similar to a unit of work designed around a research or information literacy project. The series of activities allow for demonstration and discussion of how different aspects of language or literacy can be made explicit at each step in the process. The activities are easily adapted for classroom practice. In the workshops, participants completed an accelerated version of the process; in a classroom, the process would be carried out over several days.

The initial stage of the activity is selection of a topic of interest, then thorough exploration of the field before supporting students' decisions on their own particular line of study. The topic I chose was rabbits. In addition to providing opportunities for the explicit teaching of language skills, the topic can be linked to studies of society and the environment and to science.

The steps in the process are outlined in the Table, with examples of the activities the students undertook and the related understandings the teacher chose to make explicit at each stage in the process. What needs to be made explicit will depend on what students already know and understand, which will vary in different classrooms. Each of the steps in the process is described. In addition, the following learning processes should accompany each stage:

- Explanations about why you are asking them to participate in particular activities
- Examples and demonstrations of the points you wish to make
- Time to reflect on and talk about the skills and mental processes students use to engage with the task.

TABLE   Processes for a Research-Based Unit

PROCESS	STUDENTS' ACTIVITIES	STUDENTS' UNDERSTANDINGS
Draw what you already know about this topic.	Use prior knowledge.	Learning starts with reviewing what you know.
Discuss and compare what you know using your drawings as prompts.	Learn through interaction with others (can be in home language).	Talk is an important part of learning. Learning is a social activity.
Reflect as a whole group: How do we know what we know?	Develop effective ways to reflect on learning.	Information sources can be compared and critiqued. There are many different sources of information.
Identify key words.	Predict, check, and confirm learning.	Spelling is an integral part of words.
Research: Gather further information.	Collect and analyze a range of different information. Read many different texts on the topic.	Learning takes place over time. Learning is cumulative. Reading different texts on the same topic helps improve reading.
Generate new questions.	Find relevant information to compare, interpret, and challenge.	Learning something new often causes new questions to arise.
Share what we have learned.	Describe, explain, and compare new information.	Discussion and interaction assist understanding.
Organize what we know.	Create categories for the information gathered.	Information needs to be categorized if it is to be remembered and used.
Compose a text in groups.	Build on each other's thoughts, work together, reread often, discuss, compare, and try different options.	Collaboration is a powerful, effective, and productive strategy. Reading involves a complex interaction of reading strategies. Develop reading skills.
Culmination: Produce and illustrate completed text.	Decide the purpose and genre of the text to be composed as a result of this unit of work.	Texts are shaped by their purpose.

These learning processes are essential if students are to develop the metalanguage for talking about and clearly understanding the learning that they achieve and the processes that they use. Such understanding leads to more control over and ownership of their learning.

Draw What You Know About the Topic

Ask participants to draw what they know about the topic (see Figure 1). In workshop sessions some teachers, like some students, are reluctant to draw. We stress that their drawings can be symbols, graphics, or rough sketches, as long as the creators can explain to others what they mean. They also may choose to label parts of their drawings.

FIGURE 1   Draw What You Know

Explain to participants that what is being made explicit is the concept that people learn best by recalling what they already know. Although this may be obvious to teachers, it is not always so for students, who may need to be told or reminded.

In the classroom asking students to review what they already know about a topic is a common starting point for research-based learning. It also enables students to focus on what they know rather than on how to write about what they know.

Discuss What You Know Using Your Drawing as a Prompt

When participants have completed their drawings, invite them to share with a partner what they know in order to learn new things from each other. What needs to be made explicit here is that learning occurs through interaction with other people. As teachers, we experience this in workshops, staff meetings, professional development sessions, and planning groups.

In the classroom, students need to experience and then talk about the insights and deepening understandings that occur when discussing and comparing information. Students with a first language other than English may choose to engage in this discussion in their first language. After the discussions, a short reflection time can be held with the whole class, in which the teacher invites students to give examples of what they learned and any questions raised when they discussed their drawings with a partner.

Begin a List of Key Words

At this stage, key words, which should be recorded (see Figure 2), are appearing in discussions. Ask participants to predict words they think might be common or recurring in a topic such as rabbits. Have them record their suggestions on sticky notes. If the spelling of some words is challenged, call for volunteers to check for correct spellings in a dictionary or other resource.

Add key words to the list throughout the stages. By developing a key-words list and initiating discussion about the spelling of particular words, teachers make explicit to students that correct spelling will be an expectation. Words can be added to class or individual spelling lists and addressed in the usual spelling activities that teachers devise in their programs such as explicit work on particular word patterns, or using look-say-cover-write-check strategies to learn correct spelling.

If students have had experiences in the linguistic structures and features of different genres or in analyzing texts from a critical perspective, at some time in the process,

FIGURE 2   Key Words

burrow	furry
herbivores	pests
furry	pet
export	hutch
virus	calicivirus
breeding	vermin
feral	habitat
kitten	warren

it is a good idea to examine the words on the spelling list and generate a discussion about words that might appear in certain kinds of texts. For example, the words *furry* or *friendly* are unlikely to appear in an expository text on rabbits as feral animals, but words like *pest*, *vermin*, or *calicivirus* may be expected.

How Do We Know What We Know?

Take time to review all the ways that participants gained prior knowledge about rabbits (see Figure 3). This usually generates a comprehensive list of different sources and discussion about how different sources yield different information for different purposes. For example, compare information from television documentaries with that of cartoons.

FIGURE 3   How Do We Know What We Know?

Pet rabbit experiences
Television—news, documentaries, cartoons
Beatrix Potter books
Going to the country
Living on a farm
Going shooting and trapping
Satellite mapping
Internet
Easter
Talking to people

This stage of the process demonstrates to participants the number of different sources for getting information. Strategies for making this explicit include having students participate in and contribute to the development of the list; telling them the reason behind this; discussing and comparing the different sources of information, perhaps categorizing them; and displaying the list for future reference.

Research: Gather Further Information

Have participants examine a wide range of texts about rabbits. Depending on the ages, year levels, or experience of students, teachers may collect a range of texts and make them available in the classroom. Or teachers could support students in brainstorming a list of likely sources of information that they could use. Possible sources include asking experts, using the library or resource center, collecting newspaper or magazine articles, viewing videos, or searching the Internet. The task is to use these resources, find information not previously known, and add it to the individual drawings.

It is a challenge for participants to find ways of graphically illustrating their new information. Many students want to take written notes, which should be discouraged at this stage because it sometimes leads to plagiarism. Explain to students that you want them to graphically or diagrammatically illustrate their new information in any way that will be remembered. This is possible even if observers cannot decipher the drawings.

This phase of the process is best spread over a week or two to allow participants time and opportunity to consult a range of resources. Tell students that the objective is to find new information or information that confirms or contradicts information already known. Make explicit the importance of using a range of resources by modeling, finding different kinds of texts, acknowledging students' resourcefulness in locating new information, and encouraging the sharing of resources. Students' attention can be drawn back to the original chart (Figure 3) for ideas about different sources of information.

What is also made explicit here is that reading texts is easier when we already know something about the topic. Students who read many different texts about rabbits find that reading gets easier because the information is the same or similar, just worded differently. Take the time to reflect on this with students and invite them to talk about their experiences in this regard.

From a critical literacy perspective, it might be appropriate for teachers to support students to collect the different texts they are using for this activity and sort them into categories. For example, in the resources I have used on this topic, there are expository texts seeking to build a case for eradication of rabbits; scientific reports describing characteristics such as species, habitat, and behavior; and procedural texts showing how to care for pet rabbits, as well as recounts of experiences with pet rabbits and letters to magazines about the subject. Explicit teaching of these critical literacy perspectives could begin by showing examples and talking with students about the ways that different kinds of texts are structured. Students could then work in small groups to compare the structures of different text types and identify words that are specific to each, as well as grammatical or organizational structures. This is an extension of the analysis of the key-words list mentioned earlier.

Generate Genuine Questions and Issues

Have participants discuss and compare their findings, which will lead to new questions and points of debate. Questions and issues are clarified and listed on a chart:

- Why do only rabbits die from calicivirus?
- Why do only 40% of rabbits get infected by myxomytosis?
- Does calicivirus make rabbits inedible?
- How long does it take 2 rabbits to produce 1,000?
- How are rabbits used in pregnancy tests?

What needs to be made explicit is that questions are not just something you have at the beginning of an investigation but arise as part of the ongoing process of learning new information about a topic. Throughout the research phase of the process, the teacher should be aware of the questions that students generate, and ensure that they become part of this growing list.

It is important at this stage to encourage students to record only the questions to which they do not know the answer. Do not allow this activity to degenerate to the point where dutiful students compose predictable questions to please the teacher. Point out to students that interesting questions often arise when conflicting information is found in different texts, or when information supplied verbally is challenged and needs to be verified by reference to an appropriate print text. When two students find conflicting pieces of information, they may need teacher help to turn these contradictions into questions. Reinforce the importance of these questions by periodically reviewing the list and by helping students to turn their thoughts and findings into questions for further investigation.

Share the Research

After allowing a reasonable time to complete their research, participants should discuss what they have learned in small groups. This is the time for those who have found answers to some of the questions posed to share their findings with others. Participants share and compare information, identify discrepancies, justify opinions, and explore interesting findings or issues that arise from the research. All this is done orally, allowing for more learning to occur.

In the classroom, the importance of learning processes that involve speculation, hypothesizing, comparing, explaining, inferring, imagining, and persuading need to be made explicit. One technique to make these aspects of language explicit is for the teacher to circulate among the students while they are talking and note the different kinds of talk that are occurring. After the discussion, the teacher reports back to the group, emphasizing the different kinds of talk that he or she witnessed and invites students to reflect on and offer examples of when they used talk in different ways.

Organize What We Know

At this stage, participants are asked to write on a sticky note one significant thing that they discovered during their research into rabbits. Twenty participants will result in 20 pieces of information. The teacher then categorizes the information by asking one student to read aloud his or her piece of information and to place it on a chart displayed for this purpose. The teacher then asks for information that would appear in the same category as the original.

For example, if the first piece of information is that rabbits bear four to eight litters per year, with three to eight young in each litter, additional information in the same category might be that at birth rabbits are helpless, hairless, and their eyes are closed.

Another common information category relates to rabbits as being environmentally unwelcome (for example, rabbits are a curse for farmers and environmentalists because they destroy bushland by eating all available vegetation).

When all pieces of information are sorted into appropriate categories, the next step is to look carefully at each of the categories and identify the kinds of texts that might be generated from the information. For example, the information about rabbits' breeding habits might be incorporated into a report about rabbits, and the notes about rabbits being a curse to farmers might form the basis for a piece of expository or persuasive writing to support efforts to eradicate rabbits from Australia.

In the classroom, what is made explicit at this stage is the process of creating categories by examining the information that has been collected. This is an important part of the research process in the real world, though not always made explicit in school. The teacher demonstrates and talks about this process, and the students discuss and suggest various categories until all information has been sorted appropriately.

Compose a Text in Groups

In the workshop, teachers usually identify four or five different categories of information. Each category is given to a group, which works together to construct an appropriate text, using the information given and any further information that they believe is appropriate. Categories of texts that have been identified and then worked on in workshops include expositions, reports, recounts, stories, poems, and procedures. Titles included for different genres are as follows:

Exposition:	The calicivirus: friend or foe?
Report:	The rabbit
Recount:	Adventures with my father
Story:	Hip-hop's adventure
Poem:	Rabbits
Procedure:	How to find information about rabbits on the Internet.

In the classroom, this activity is a variation on the strategy known as *joint construction of text* and is used to give students support when attempting different text types or genres. Some teachers may prefer to select only one of the possible text types for focused attention, which will manage the explicit teaching of the required skills more effectively. Others may find it appropriate to allow students to work on texts in genres of their own choosing. In either case, before students commence work on their text, they will need support in deciding on a purpose or use for the finished product. For example, an expository text on the use-of-calicivirus issue could be developed as a letter to the editor of a local newspaper; a report about rabbits could be prepared as a Big Book for junior primary classes; or a procedural text on how to find information on the Internet could be displayed in the resource center for other users.

Culmination: Produce and Illustrate Completed Text

In the classroom, the texts that students produce should be edited, polished, and used for whatever purposes have been decided previously. For example, the letter to the editors can be sent to the newspaper, and the report prepared for junior primary students presented and read during a school assembly. Although the finished product is important, the significant learning occurred during the explicit teaching sessions the teacher planned and presented throughout the process. The teachers experience a process in the workshop that can be adapted to their own classroom situations, depending on the age and experience of students.

Related Explicit Teaching Activities

The texts composed by students in small groups are an excellent resource for teachers to explicitly teach writing and reading skills. Examples of specific strategies for the teaching of particular reading and writing skills follow. These are not intended to be duplicated exercises for students to complete but are meant to be teaching aids, which are valuable because they are contextualized within the students' current experiences, knowledge, and interests. They enable teachers to demonstrate reading and writing strategies through texts with which the students are already familiar. The teacher can demonstrate particular language features and compare alternatives. In general, the activities give students the opportunity to engage in learning by talking, doing, and reflecting on the processes used.

Sample 1: Cloze Activity to Demonstrate Use of Prior Knowledge in Reading

This activity demonstrates to students that prior knowledge of a topic can be used to predict the meaning of words they do not know. The teacher has taken part of a student-generated text and deleted a number of content words (Sample 1). The text is then shown on an overhead transparency. The class is invited to identify missing words using their knowledge of this topic. Discussion follows on how they worked out the missing words and the application of this strategy in normal reading.

Rabbits

Wild _____ live in underground _____ called warrens. Sometimes there are hundreds of rabbits in the same _____ of warrens.

They do not go far from their warrens. When they sense _____ they make for the nearest _____ entrance.

Rabbits are hunted by many _____ as well as by humans.

Apart from humans, the rabbit's _____ are _____ , eagles, and _____ .

Rabbits can sit perfectly still in the hope of not being _____ but when chased can move speedily over _____ distances.

They are most active between _____ and _____ .

Sample 2: Explicit Teaching of the Use of Pronouns

A female rabbit is called a doe.

_____ babies are called kittens.

_____ carries _____ babies in

_____ body for 4 weeks

before _____ are born.

Sample 2 is an example of an activity that focuses on the use of pronouns. After some discussion of pronouns and perhaps some examples from other texts, a cloze activity (Sample 3) helps students further clarify their understandings. Transferring the text to an overhead transparency and inviting the class to predict the missing words allows for discussion and for students to articulate reasons for their choices of particular pronouns. This is important in learning to talk about language and learning to use language.

Sample 3: A Read-Aloud Cloze Activity Focusing on Vowel Sounds

In spr_ng and s_mmer

r_bbits may g_ve birth

every 4 or 5 weeks.

This is the kind of text that might be used with beginning readers and writers to help them understand and discriminate between vowel sounds. Because only short texts are appropriate for this activity, teachers can prepare these examples quickly and easily in response to individual students' needs. Alternatively, this strategy can be used with small groups of students, using large sheets of paper and colored texts.

Sample 4: Sentence Manipulation to Learn About Sentence Elements

A rabbit	licks its paws	and runs them	over its ears	to wash them.

Sample 4 strategy consists of writing a sentence on a strip of cardboard and cutting the sentence into parts so it can be reconstructed by the teacher to demonstrate and talk about various elements of a sentence: subject/verb/object, how phrases fit together, or how to use pronouns correctly. Depending on the teaching focus, a sentence might be cut into individual words or phrases.

Sample 5: Sentence Extension Activities

Original or core sentence:

The doe digs a nest and lines it with grass and fur.

Extended sentence:

In the wild, the doe digs a nest and lines it with grass and her own soft fur, which she pulls out with her teeth.

In Sample 5, the teacher prepares a basic sentence, cuts it into parts, and has students suggest and insert phrases and parts of speech to extend the sentence. This allows opportunities for talking about different ways of manipulating language to make it more effective or interesting. Who, where, when, what, or why questions are used to encourage suggestions from students.

Using the Four Literacy Roles Framework

The unit of work described shows how explicit teaching can occur in a number of different aspects of literacy, including using and valuing prior knowledge, technical skills of spelling and grammar, understandings about multiple sources of information, and recognition of the benefits of collaborative learning and identification of different text types and their purposes. Teachers need to regularly review their literacy teaching to ensure that students are given access to a broad and balanced literacy program, with explicit teaching of whatever aspects are needed to be taught explicitly to particular students.

The model of four roles of a literate person (See Figure 4; see also Chapter 7) (Freebody & Luke, 1990) provides a framework for analysis of the rabbits unit of work, as well as other learning activities.

The *code-breaker* role focuses on the technical skills that a learner needs. These skills are reflected in the key-words list and in the explicit teaching activities designed around the texts that students compose.

The *text-participant* role focuses on learners being able to draw from their experiences and interpretations of events and use these as a starting place for new learning.

FIGURE 4 Four Roles of a Literate Person

CODE BREAKER	TEXT PARTICIPANT
How do I crack this code?	What does this mean to me?
Emphasis on rules and skills	Emphasis on the knowledge or interpretation of the topic that the participant brings to the text
Some connections to traditional approaches to literacy teaching	Some connections to whole language approaches to literacy teaching
TEXT USER	**TEXT ANALYST**
What do I do with this text?	What does this text do to me?
Emphasis on the purposes and uses of different texts and how purpose shapes texts	Emphasis on the concept that ideas and information in texts are not neutral and can be challenged
Some connections to genre approaches to literacy teaching	Some connections to critical approaches to literacy teaching

This is evident at the commencement of the work, where participants are asked to draw on their experiences with rabbits.

The *text-user* role focuses on learners understanding the uses of texts and the ways in which purpose shapes the structure and language of text. This is highlighted in the stage when participants sort information into categories and identify the kinds of texts that might be appropriate for them to write.

Finally, the *text-analyst* role foregrounds the critical elements of literacy, which require learners to consider how the text positions particular persons or groups. Analysis of some of the different texts that participants encounter during the research stage of the process provides opportunities to consider and compare different perspectives on rabbits that are reflected by different writers.

Conclusion

Teachers in these workshops have translated this unit into classroom practice for students from preschool to Year 12. Kindergartners also have been involved in the first stages of the process. Provided the topic is one that they are interested in and have some prior knowledge about, kindergartners can draw what they know, share this with a friend, talk about how they know what they know, and add more information or make a new drawing when they learn new things about the topic.

Teachers in the workshop leave with new enthusiasm to try the process with their students. Many different topics have been used, which span most areas of the curriculum and are based on the interests of students and the requirements of the areas of study. Teachers adapt the process for their own needs, and spend varying amounts of time on the different aspects, depending on what needs to be made explicit for particular groups of students.

Whatever the topic or area of study, teachers find the process useful to make previously invisible learning outcomes and processes explicit for students by demonstrating literacy strategies; providing opportunities for active participation; talking with students about their literacy learning strategies; and supporting students in developing the metalanguage of analysis and reflection, which they require to talk, think about, and use language.

References

Delpit, L. (1988). The silenced dialogue: Power and pedagogy in educating other people's children. *Harvard Educational Review, 58*, 280–298.

McConnell, S. (1993). Talking drawings: A strategy for assisting learners. *Journal of Reading, 6*(4), 260–269.

Freebody P., & Luke, A. (1990). Literacies' programs: Debates and demands in cultural contexts. *Prospect: Journal of Adult Migrant Education Programs, 5*(3), 7–16.

Reflections on a Teacher Research Group: A Leap Forward

Joelie Hancock

When I began this research project, my aim was to document explicit-teaching classroom practices. The teachers and I documented these practices in teaching reading, and we all became much clearer about what it means to teach explicitly, but we achieved much more. The teachers advanced as confident, professional leaders, and experienced the struggle of revision in writing. We all learned the power of taking time to reflect and share ideas with others. I learned that by continually recalling classroom decisions and events, many layers of complexity are revealed.

The research was characterized by efforts to be as clear as possible. (This surprised some of the teachers, who thought that research was more about taking different measures of achievement and opinion and comparing the results.) There were three distinct phases in our operation as a research group, whose role was to put into words and make clear to one another what we wanted to achieve, what we did, and what we accomplished:

1. Clarify what we wanted to do.

2. Implement our plans (and reflect).

3. Report (and reflect).

The first two phases each took one school term, and we met approximately once a month on Saturday mornings. The last phase took about one month, as the teachers prepared and reported their findings to other teachers at a professional development day. Ideally, the last phase should continue as long as the teachers have opportunities to orally report to other teachers or revise their written reports for different audiences. Each teacher presented her research orally two to six times and three times in writing.

Getting It Clear

An essential part of teachers' becoming clear about what they wanted to do was bouncing ideas off one another and reading about the approaches and insights of other teachers. The other crucial part was to have time to think, plan, and write. At our first meetings, we discussed the different understandings of what explicit teaching meant, why we thought explicit teaching was important, and some explicit teaching strategies that we might implement. Through these discussions, we constructed and agreed on the following:

> Explicit teaching involves making clear to learners what they are learning, how they can learn it, and how they will know when they are successful. Teachers discussed various strategies already in use to make learning clear to their students and other strategies that teachers were using to make learning clear in their classrooms. These strategies included providing choice for students (Weeks, 1987), teacher-student negotiation (Boomer, 1982), and demonstrations with think-alouds (Hancock & Leaver, 1993). Articles were available if the teachers wanted to read more about any of the strategies.

The teachers' first task was to identify an aspect of their students' learning in reading that they wanted to improve and to decide what they could make clearer in order to improve that learning. Over several meetings the teachers explored ideas they were considering and wrote answers to the questions listed below. Some of this exploration was accomplished by everyone in writing, talking about their plans, or in individual discussions with me. Most of the teachers struggled to put into words the concerns and decisions that they were confronting every day:

- What aspect of learning am I concerned about in my reading program?
- Why is this learning important?
- How do I normally teach this?
- What will I make explicit?
- How will I make this explicit?
- What will the students be able to do better as a result?
- How will I know?
- What records will I collect?
- What support will I need?

At one meeting, as well as clarifying their individual projects, the teachers were introduced to the notion of *interactive trouble* (Freebody, Ludwig, & Gunn, 1994; see also the Preface of this volume). Interactive trouble refers to the miscommunications that occur in classrooms between the teacher and students when "students do not cue into the perspective represented in the teacher's talk" (p. 297). The teachers found this concept useful in examining and describing some of the interactions in their classrooms. They discussed how teachers often have in their minds a process and answers, which may not have been at all clear to the students. Often students' *wrong* answers are perfectly logical, but are dismissed by the teacher. Often the teacher has a purpose for an activity and definite expectations, but by not making these clear, students are left uncertain about what they are meant to do and have little motivation to do it.

Another idea discussed was how teachers might capitalize on students' current understandings, purposes, and motivations by bringing into the classroom program the interests, texts, and literacy activities that students already valued. Such activities and texts would be meaningful to the students, because they would be already familiar with the contexts in which these texts were used and with their functions. For example, they already knew that magazines are entertaining, informative, easy to read, and used for relaxation. This knowledge that students bring from their families to schools we referred to as *cultural capital*, a notion explored by Bourdieu (1986) and Moll et al. (1992).

At monthly meetings and sometimes through exchanges of faxes, teachers shared and developed their plans so they could be ready to teach them in the next term.

Classroom Implementation

This phase of the research—the central, essential part—was the least time consuming and difficult. Having planned so thoroughly what they wanted to teach and how they would do it, and being clearer than usual about what they wanted to achieve, the teaching passed effortlessly. None of the teachers took audio or video recordings of what happened, and most relied on their planning notes and the students' work to reconstruct what had occurred for their reports.

Reporting

Although much of the clarifying was done in the planning stage of the project, most of the teachers' learning was accomplished by reporting: first to the other researchers in the group, then to other teachers in workshops, and then to other teachers in writing. As one teacher said in a year-end group meeting, "Through talking and writing and reflecting, I refined my thinking and teaching. Writing made me reflect on what I was doing in the classroom."

In working with the teachers with their individual writing, I found that I was challenging them about their practice simply by saying "It's not clear here how the students knew what to do," or asking "Why do you think the students did that?" or "Were your students able to achieve that?" Although I could see that the teachers often had to think hard about what was really going on in their classrooms, they found this rewarding. One teacher said,

> It's good to be challenged, to question whether I am achieving what I set out to do. I have become more aware of whether I am making the learning clear enough to my students.

Not only did the teachers learn about their teaching through this reflection and reporting process, but they learned about writing: that "it takes a long time," it requires a lot of rewriting and revision, "how to find an appropriate register," how to format a written report, and how to "cater to another audience." The pleasure at having a final published paper also was expressed by one of the teachers:

> I don't often complete things in a formal format. I'm used to my stuff being in draft on pad paper. It was actually a very nice feeling to see it all typed up. Knowing something I've written will appear in a teacher journal makes me feel brilliant! It's encouraged me to seriously consider completing a masters degree.

Other Important Elements

An important element in the success of the teachers' research was meeting at regular times. Research shows that teachers benefit from time away from the classroom to reflect on aspects of their teaching and to talk about their successes and their concerns with other teachers. These experienced teachers already knew this before they committed the time. As one teacher commented,

> When I have time to reflect and bounce ideas off others, my teaching takes a leap forward.

Others reported that having the 6-month time frame gave them a clear, definable focus; meeting monthly meant that they kept working on their writing between sessions; and having a shared context of topic and task was helpful. Another aspect of this project that several of the teachers appreciated was the chance to share ideas with others teaching at different levels. They made the comments that follow:

> It was good to see the bigger picture—reception to secondary.
> I felt valued by other levels of teaching.

The teachers also gained a better appreciation of the work they were doing in their classrooms. One teacher said,

I often underestimate the significance of what I'm doing in my classroom. By sharing, I come to value what I am doing.

They also gained confidence and recognized the pleasure of sharing their class-room practice with others. Another teacher commented,

What I've done has opened doors for other teachers. I've really enjoyed doing a variety of workshop sessions to share the proformas developed and the results of working with this strategy.

Conclusion

This project had very modest beginnings. It developed from the small goal of planning and presenting teachers' classroom explorations to other interested teachers. To support that goal, we needed to be clear about what we wanted to do and what we had learned. By talking among ourselves and making clear to one another what we were doing, we found ourselves having to reflect on our planning, our thinking, our classroom messages, and our writing. Every teaching moment is made up of such reflections. It is rare, however, that we reflect on our teaching moments in ways that force us to put into words what we are doing and achieving. Through making explicit our teaching and its achievements, the teachers in this project were able to take a leap forward.

References
Boomer, G. (1994). Negotiating the curriculum reformulated. In G. Boomer, N. Lester, C. Onore, & J. Cook (Eds.), *Negotiating the curriculum: Educating for the 21st century* (pp. 276–289). London: Falmer Press.
Bourdieu, P. (1986). The forms of capital. In J.G. Richardson (Ed.), *Handbook of theory and research for the sociology of education* (pp. 241–258). New York: Greenwood Press.
Freebody, P., Ludwig, C., & Gunn, S. (1995). Everyday literacy practices in and out of school. In *Children's Literacy National Project* (Vol. 1., pp. 297–315). Adelaide, SA: Department of Education, Employment and Training.
Hancock, J., & Leaver, C. (1994). *Major teaching strategies for English*. Carlton, VIC: Australian Reading Association.
Moll, L., Armanti, C., Neff, D., & Gonzalez, N. (1992). Funds of knowledge for teaching: Using a qualitative approach to connect homes and classrooms. *Theory Into Practice, 31*(2), 132–141.
Weeks, B. (1987). Structuring for choice. In J. Hancock & B. Comber (Eds.), *Independent learners* (pp. 136–150). North Ryde, NSW: Methuen Australia.

Index

Page references followed by *n*, *t* or *f* indicate notes, tables, or figures, respectively.

A

ABORIGINAL EDUCATION UNIT (Adelaide), 47*n*1

ACHIEVEMENT: assigning levels of, 96*n*1; student, 78; Using Student Achievement Data to Improve Student Learning Outcomes project, 81

ACQUISITION: subconscious, 3–7; via immersion and demonstration, 7

ACTIVITIES: clarification of, viii; cloze, 121–122; presentation, 59, 59*f*; read-aloud cloze, 122; related, 121–123; sentence extension, 123

AHANG, SALLY, viii, 49–61

ALEA. *See* Australian Literacy Educators' Association

ALL THE BETTER TO SEE YOU WITH, 33

ALLOWAY, N., 4, 10

ANALYZING MEDIA, 34–36

ANCIENT GREECE (TOPIC): concept map on, 100, 100*f*; explicitly introducing, 100–101; student travel brochures, 106, 107*f*-108*f*

ANSTEY, M., 10–11

ANSWERS: different, 13–28; wrong, 128

APPRENTICESHIP, 6

ARMANTI, C., 130

ASSESSMENT, 67–70, 70*f*, 72; by asking students, 106, 109; of diagrams, 69–70, 71*f*; of expression, 76–78; for student portfolio, 68*f*, 68–69; Summary Sheet, 76, 77*f*; tasks for, 72

ASSESSMENT CRITERIA, 106; introducing, 106

ASSESSMENT SHEET, 72, 75*f*

ASSISTANCE: in reading magazines at home, 44, 44*f*

AUSTRALIAN LITERACY EDUCATORS' ASSOCIATION (ALEA), vi

AUSTRALIAN READING ASSOCIATION COUNCIL, vi

B

BADGER, L., 4, 8, 11

BAKER, JEANNIE, 66, 68*f*

BALANCED CURRICULUM, 6

BIG BOOKS: class work with, 72; format, 13–14; *Point of View*, 14; reasons for using, 14

Big Buddies, 32

"THE BLIND MEN AND THE ELEPHANT," 25

BOOK CYCLES: data analysis, 60; organizational information for, 55, 55*f*

BOOKS: asking students about finding, 98–99; children's, 37; comparing with magazines, 42–46; for discovering layers of meaning in texts, 31–34; why students choose to read, 43; why students prefer, 43; written responses to, 58*f*, 58–59

BOOMER, G., 127, 130

BOTTOM STORY, viii

BOURDIEU, P., 128, 130

BRAINSTORMING, viii

BROCHURES: travel, 105–106, 107*f*–108*f*

BROWN, A.L., 8, 12

C

CAMBOURNE, B., 4, 11
CAPITAL: cultural, 39–48, 128
CARRINGTON, V., 44, 48
CHARTED LIST, 67, 68
CHILDREN'S BOOKS, 37
CHRISTIE, FRANCES, 2
CLARK, REBECCA, 97
CLASSROOM: cohesive, productive, 47; implementation in, 128; pedagogy of, 5–6; as publishing room, 46–47; strategies that support and enhance exploring layers of meaning in text in, 36–37. *See also* School
CLEMENT, ROD, 66, 68*f*
CLOZE ACTIVITIES: to demonstrate use of prior knowledge in reading, 121–122; read-aloud, 122–123
CLYNE, M., 5, 11
CODE BREAKER ROLE, 86, 87*f*–88*f*, 124, 124*f*
COMBER, B., vi, x, 1–2, 11
COMMUNICATION: with parents, 63
COMPETENCE: increased, 5
COMPOSITION OF TEXT: in groups, 120–121
CONNELL, R.W., 2, 11
CONSCIOUS LEARNING, 3–7
CONSTRUCTION OF TEXT: joint, 120
CONTEXTUALIZED LEARNING, 48*n*1
CORMACK, P., vi, x
CORNERSTONES: TRAINING AND DEVELOPMENT PROGRAM, vi, x, 29, 37, 85, 87*f*–88*f*, 96
CULTURAL CAPITAL, 44, 128; building on, 39–48
CULTURES OF POWER, 112
CUMMING, J.J., 11
CURRICULUM: balanced, 6; *English—A Curriculum Profile for Australian Schools*, 96*n*1
CURRICULUM CORPORATION, 96

D

DAHL, K.L., 6, 11
DECS. *See* Department of Education and Children's Services
DELPIT, LISA D., vii, x, 2, 11, 112, 125
DEMONSTRATION: acquisition via, 7
DEPARTMENT OF EDUCATION AND CHILDREN'S SERVICES (DECS), 48*n*1, 50
DIAGRAMS: assessment of, 69–70, 71*f*; interpreting and creating, 69–70; student work sample of criteria for, 68–69, 70*f*
DISCOURSES, 3; kinds of, 3; primary, 3; secondary, 3
DISCUSSION: with drawings as prompts, 116
DOIG, S.M., 11
DRAWING(S), 69; as discussion prompts, 115; talking, 113; about topics, 115, 115*f*

E

EARLY YEARS LITERACY TEAM, 113
EDUCATION DEPARTMENT OF WESTERN AUSTRALIA, 36
EDWARDS, MEREDITH, ix, 80–96
ELIOT, T.S., 62–63, 64*f*, 79; objectives for work with, 76

ENGLISH TEACHERS: questions that concern, 81

ENGLISH—A CURRICULUM PROFILE FOR AUSTRALIAN SCHOOLS, 96n1

EPISTEMOLOGICAL TROUBLE, 91

EVELINE, J., 2, 11

EXPECTATIONS: clarification of, viii

EXPLANATORY LETTERS TO PARENTS, 63, 65*f*

EXPLICIT TASK SHEET, 109, 110*f*

EXPLICIT TEACHING, vi, 112–125, 127; concerns about, 9–10; definition of, vi–vii, 80, 97; insights about, 93–95; introduction to, 1–12; learning via, 7; with literature circles, 49–61; metacognition in, 7–8; processes and strategies with literature circles, 49–61; related activities, 121–123; strategies for, 113; strategies that support and enhance exploring layers of meaning in text, 36–37; of use of pronouns, 122

EXPLICIT TEACHING OF READING PROJECT: setting up, 82; teacher response to, 93–95

EXPLICITLY INTRODUCING TOPICS, 100–101

EXPLICITLY TEACHING READING OF NONFICTION TEXTS, 97–111; assessment of, 106; completed student travel brochures, 106, 107*f*-108*f*; future directions, 109; halfway stage, 103–104; halfway-stage questionnaire, 104*t*, 104–105, 105*t*; lessons learned, 109; progress summary, 104; steps, 98–103, 104–109; unit stages, 98

EXPLICITLY TEACHING TRAVEL BROCHURE FEATURES, 105–106

EXPRESSION: appropriate, 76; assessment of, 76–78; lesson sequence, 76; Summary Sheet, 76, 77*f*

F

FICTION: focus on, 49–50

FIRST STEPS, 33

FOX, MEM, 27, 71; *Wilfred Gordon McDonald Partridge*, 18–20

FREEBODY, P., ix, vi, vii, x, 5, 7, 11–12, 29, 37, 42, 48, 85, 87*f*-88*f*, 91, 96, 124–125, 128, 130

FREPPON, P.A., 6, 11

G

GEE, JAMES, vii, x, 1, 3, 5–6, 11

GEHLING, KERRY, viii, 62–79

GENRE APPROACH, 2

GILBERT, P., 4, 10

GONZALEZ, N., 130

GOODMAN, K.S., 4, 11

GRAHAM, BOB, 38; *Rose Meets Mr. Wintergarten*, 30–31, 31*f*

GREEN, B., 1, 11

GROUP DISCUSSION: with drawings as prompts, 116

GROUPS, 67; composing text in, 120–121; creating, 53–59; small, 61; working with literature texts in, 61

GUNN, S., vi, x, 11, 41, 47, 88, 96, 128, 130

H

HALLIDAY, M.A.K., 5, 11

HANCOCK, JOELIE, vi–x, 8, 11, 126–130

HEADINGS: teaching use of, 102

HERSCHELL, P., 10, 12

HODGENS, J., 1, 11

HOLDAWAY, D., 4, 11

HOME: linking to school with popular texts, 39–48; popular texts read at, 40–41, 41*f*; reading magazines at, 44, 44*f*

I

ILLUSTRATION(S): of completed texts, 121; role of, 66–69; teaching use of, 102
IMMERSION: acquisition via, 6
INFORMATION: gathering further, 117–118; organizing, 119–120; sources for, 117, 117*f*; from titles, 30–31, 31*f*
INFORMATION TEXTS: finding main points in, 72, 73*f*; main points in, 70–72. *See also* Text(s)
INTELLIGENCE(S): multiple, 52
INTERACTIVE TROUBLE, vii, 91, 128

J

JANKS, H., 8, 11
JOCKEY: point of view with, 25–26
JOHNSTON, K.M., 2, 11
JOINT CONSTRUCTION OF TEXT, 120
JORGENSEN, GAIL, 66, 68*f*
JOURNALS: reading strategy, 91–93
JOYCE, BERNIE, 72, 79

K

KEEFE, C.H., 50, 61
KEY WORDS LISTS, 116–117, 116*f*
KNOWLEDGE IN READING: prior, 121–122

L

LAND BEFORE TIME, 32
LAYERS OF MEANING IN TEXTS: analyzing media, 34–37; benefits of exploring, 36; books for discovering, 32–34; classroom strategies that support and enhance exploring, 36–37; discovering, 31–34; exploring, 29–38; information from titles, 30–31, 31*f*; questions for discovering, 33; reflections on exploring, 37
LEARNING: clarification of activities, viii; conscious, 3–7; contextualized, 48*n*1; four roles of learners, 85–86, 87*f*–88*f*, 124–125; literacy, vi–vii; processes for research-based unit, 113–114, 114*t*; about sentence elements, 123; via explicit teaching, 7
LEAVER, C., 8, 11, 127, 130
LESSONS: reading, 63–66; sequence for expression, 76
LETTERS: explanatory, 63, 65*f*; parent, 78
LINGARD, B., 1, 11
LINKING HOME AND SCHOOL LITERACIES WITH POPULAR TEXTS, 39–48; books vs magazines for, 42–46; classroom as publishing room for, 46–47; focus on magazines, 41–42; lessons learned, 48; preliminary survey, 40*f*, 40–41; teaching implications, 47–48
LITERACY LEARNING: theories and related practices, vi–vii
LITERACY ROLES, 85–86, 87*f*–88*f*; using framework of, 124–125
LITERACY SETS, 1
LITERATURE APPRECIATION: objectives, 63–66
LITERATURE CIRCLES, 49–61, 69; achievement, 60–61; creating groups, 53–59; data analysis, 60–61; explicit processes and strategies with, 49–61; final presentation activities, 59, 59*f*; final written book

responses, 56, 58*f*; future directions, 61; goal, 50; introducing novels, 53–59; monitoring students' participation, 59; opportunities for students, 60–61; organizational information for reading cycles, 55, 55*f*; outcomes, strategies, and resources, 51*t*–52*t*; Paragraph Planning Sheet, 56, 59*f*; procedures, 50–53; questions to answer in, 69; Reading Checklist, 53, 54*f*; stickums, 55, 56*f*; student selection sheet for, 53*f*; Teacher's Monitoring Sheet, 59, 60*f*; weekly timetable, 59, 60*f*
literature texts: in small groups, 61. *See also* Text(s)
LoBianco, J., 12
Ludwig, C., vi, x, 10–12, 42, 48, 91, 96, 128, 130
Luke, A., ix, x, 1–2, 7, 11, 29, 37, 44, 48, 85, 87*f*–88*f*, 96, 124–125
luxury: points of view about, 26–27, 27*f*

M

magazines: comparing with books, 42–46; elements of, 41, 41*f*; focus on, 41–42; reading at home, 44, 44*f*; *Teddy Magazine*, 41–42, 47; what students look at first in, 44, 44*f*; why students choose to read, 43; why students prefer, 43
main points: in information text, 71, 73*f*; reading and reporting, 70
Marshall, Jay, ix, 97–111
Martin, Jim, 2
Matthews, Lynda, viii, 29–38
McConnell, Suzanne, 113, 125
McGrath, H., 51*t*, 52, 61
meaning in texts: layers of, 29–38
media analysis, 33–35; questions for, 34–35
metacognition, 7–8; for teachers and students, 80–96
Moll, L., 128, 130
monitoring: observation checklist for, 86, 89*f*–90*f*; of student participation, 59; Teacher's Monitoring Sheet, 59, 60*f*
Morgan, W., 8, 12
motivation, 14; strategies that support and enhance exploring layers of meaning in text, 35
Mullins, Patricia, 66, 68*f*, 72
multiple intelligences, 52
Munro, John, 83, 85, 96
Munro, Kate, 83, 85, 96
My Dearest Dinosaur (Wild), 31

N

National Schools Network, 46, 48*n*2
NCP. *See* Negotiated Curriculum Plan
Neff, D., 130
Negotiated Curriculum Plan (NCP), 93, 96*n*1
newspaper photos: point of view with, 17
Nixon, H., 11
Noble, T., 50*t*, 51, 60
nonfiction texts: explicitly teaching reading of, 97–111
Norton, D.E., 8, 12
note taking: asking students about, 98–99; explicit strategies for, 109–111; on sticky notes, 101, 101*f*; teaching, 101; teaching use of headings, subheadings, topic sentences, and illustrations when, 102
notes: framework for, 102, 103*f*; teaching how to build into framework, 102–103
novels: introducing, 53–59

NURSERY RHYMES: point of view in, 14–15, 15*f*

O

O'BRIEN, J., 8, 12
OBSERVATION CHECKLIST, 86, 89*f*–90*f*
O'NEILL, KAREN, 93–94
ORGANIZATION OF INFORMATION, 119–120
ORGANIZATIONAL INFORMATION: for reading cycles, 55, 55*f*
ORGANIZATIONAL TROUBLE, 91
O'SULLIVAN, CUSHLA, 94

P

PAIRWORK, 65–66
PALINCSAR, A.S., vi, x, 8, 12
PARAGRAPH PLANNING SHEET, 56, 57*f*
PARENTS: communication with, 63; explanatory letter to, 63, 65*f*; letter and questionnaire for, 78
PARIS, S., vi, x
PARTICIPATION: monitoring, 59, 60*f*
PEDAGOGY: classroom, 5–6
PETER (BART SIMPSON'S COUSIN): point of view with Peter, a bee, and a flower, 21–22
PICTURES: role of, 66–69
PITT, J., 11
POINT OF VIEW: "The Blind Men and the Elephant," 25; definition of, 18–19; exploring, 13–28; final
    reflections, 27–28; goals for students, 13–14; with house for sale, 20; with houses for sale, 26; with
    jockey, 25–26; lunch-time dilemma, 22; about luxury, 26–27, 27*f*; with man in danger, 18–19;
    with morning glory and Wilfred Gordon, 19–20, 19*f*; in newspaper photos, 18; in nursery rhymes,
    14–15, 15*f*; with Peter, a bee, and a flower, 21–22, 21*f*; with play equipment, 15–17, 16*f*; research
    project, 13–28; with sprouting potato, 23*f*, 22–25, 24*f*
POINT OF VIEW BIG BOOK, 14
POND, ROY, 52
POPULAR TEXTS: linking home and school literacies with, 39–48; read at home, 40–41, 41*f*; read at
    school, 40*f*, 40–41. *See also* Text(s)
POWER: cultures of, 112
PRACTICALITY, 14
PRESENTATION ACTIVITIES: final, 59, 59*f*
PRIOR KNOWLEDGE IN READING: cloze activity to demonstrate, 121–122
PROFESSIONAL DEVELOPMENT, 93–95
PRONOUNS: explicit teaching of use of, 122
PUBLISHING: classroom as room for, 46–47; *Teddy Magazine*, 46–47; workshop, viii

Q

QUESTIONNAIRE: parent, 78
QUESTIONS AND ISSUES: clarifying, 118–119; generating, 118–119

R

READ-ALOUD CLOZE ACTIVITY: focusing on vowel sounds, 122–123
READERS, 99–100; as text analysts, 86, 87*f*–88*f*, 124, 124*f*; as text decoders, 86, 87*f*–88*f*, 124, 124*f*; as
    text participants, 86, 87*f*–88*f*, 124, 124*f*; as text users, 86, 87*f*–88*f*, 124, 124*f*

READING, 3; asking students about, 98–99; of books, 41–42; explicit teaching of, 1–12; at home, 39–40, 41*f*; of magazines, 42–43; of magazines at home, 44, 44*f*; of main points, 71; prior knowledge in, 121–122; at school, 40*f*, 40–41; sustained silent, 49; teaching, 7, 82–83; types of, 47

READING CHECKLIST, 53, 54*f*

READING CIRCLES. *See* Literature circles

READING CYCLES: data analysis, 60–61; organizational information for, 55, 55*f*

READING GROUPS, 67. *See also* Groups

READING LESSONS, 63–66

READING NONFICTION TEXTS: explicitly teaching, 97–111

READING PROGRAM, 62–79; final reflections, 79; lesson sequence, 76; lessons, 66–72; objectives, 66–72, 76; parent comments, 78–79; parent letter and questionnaire, 78; student achievement, 78

READING STRATEGIES, 83–86, 102–103; after-reading, 85; before-reading, 83–84; to develop reading skills, 99–100; during-reading, 84; to help become better readers, 83–86; to help understand reading, 84–85; to prepare for reading, 83–84; remembering, 85; teaching, 82–83

READING STRATEGY JOURNALS: example comments, 92; role of, 91–93

REFLECTION, 129–130

REID, J., 8, 12

RELATED EXPLICIT TEACHING ACTIVITIES, 121–124; culmination, 123–124; samples, 121–123

REPORTING, 128–129; of main points, 71

RESEARCH, 117–118; asking students about, 98–99; objectives, 63–66; point of view, 13–28; sharing, 119; strategies for, 72, 74*f*; teacher groups, 126–130; unit processes, 113–114, 114*t*

REVISITS, 14

RODDA, EMILY, 51

ROSE MEETS MR. WINTERGARTEN (Graham), 30–31, 31*f*

ROTHERY, JOAN, 2

RUBINSTEIN, GILLIAN, 52

RYAN, J., 11

S

SAWYER, R., 101, 111

SCHOOL: linking to home with popular texts, 39–48; popular texts read at, 40*f* 40–41. *See also* Classroom

SCOTT, JANINE, 72, 79

SENTENCES: extension activities, 123; manipulation to learn about elements of, 123; topic, 70, 102

SHARING IDEAS, 129–130

SHARING RESEARCH, 119

SHEPHERD, LYN, viii, 39–48

SILENT READING: sustained, 50; variations in, 47

SIMPSON, A., 50, 60*f*, 61

SIMPSON, BART: point of view with Peter (his cousin), a bee, and a flower, 21–22

SMALL GROUPS: working with literature texts in, 61. *See also* Groups

SMITH, JUDY, vii, 13–28

SPIELBERG, S., 38

SSR. *See* Sustained silent reading

STEPTOE, JOHN, 66, 68*f*

STICKUMS, 55, 56*f*

STICKY NOTES, 101, 101*f*

STINE, R.L., 61

STORY: bottom, viii; top, viii

Index

STUCKEY, J.E., 1–2, 12

STUDENT PORTFOLIO: assessment for, 68*f*, 68–69; assessment of diagrams for, 69–70, 71*f*

STUDENT TRAVEL BROCHURES, 105, 107*f*–108*f*

STUDENT WORK SAMPLES, 67*f*, 67–69; of criteria for diagram, 69–70, 70*f*

STUDENTS: assessment of approach by asking, 106–109; metacognition for, 80–96; in pairs, 66

STYLISTIC TROUBLE, 91

SUBCONSCIOUS ACQUISITION, 3–7

SUBHEADINGS: teaching use of, 102

SUMMARY SHEET, 76, 77*f*

SUSTAINED SILENT READING, 49

SWITALA, JENNY, 94

T

TALKING DRAWINGS, 113

TEACHER RESEARCH: classroom implementation, 128; important elements, 129–130; reporting, 128–129

TEACHER RESEARCH GROUPS: phases, 126; reflections on, 126–130

TEACHERS: concerns and decisions confronted daily, 127–128; English, 81; metacognition for, 80–96; response to explicit teaching of reading project, 92–95

TEACHER'S MONITORING SHEET, 59, 60*f*

TEACHING, 6; explicit, vi–vii, 7–10, 29, 39, 49, 80, 112–125, 127; how to build notes into framework, 102–103; implications of linking home and school literacies with popular texts project, 47–48

TEACHING EXPLICITLY, vi, 29; concerns about, 9–10; definition of, vi–vii, 39, 49, 61, 80, 97; insights about, 93–95; introduction to, 1–12; learning via, 7; with literature circles, 49–61; metacognition in, 7–8; strategies that support and enhance exploring layers of meaning in text, 36–37

TEACHING NOTE TAKING, 101

TEACHING READING, 7; explicit, 1–12; training and development on strategies for, 81–82

TEACHING READING OF NONFICTION TEXTS: explicit, 97–111

TEACHING READING STRATEGY, 83

TEACHING TRAVEL BROCHURE FEATURES: explicit, 105–106

TEACHING USE OF HEADINGS, SUBHEADINGS, TOPIC SENTENCES, AND ILLUSTRATIONS WHEN TAKING NOTES, 102

TEACHING WRITING: genre approach to, 2

TEDDY MAGAZINE, 41–42; factors that helped in writing, 46; publishing, 46–47

TEXT(S), 29–30; composing in groups, 120–121; finding main points in, 71, 73*f*; information, 70–73, 73*f*; joint construction of, 120; layers of meaning in, 29–38; linking home and school literacies with, 39–48; literature, 61; main points in, 70–71; nonfiction, 97–111; popular, 39–48; producing and illustrating, 123–124; read at home, 40–41, 41*f*; read at school, 40*f*, 40–41; in small groups, 61

TEXT ANALYST ROLE, 86, 87*f*–88*f*, 124*f*, 124

TEXT DECODER ROLE, 86, 87*f*–88*f*, 124*f*, 124

TEXT PARTICIPANT ROLE, 86, 87*f*–88*f*, 124*f*, 124

TEXT USER ROLE, 86, 87*f*–88*f*, 124*f*, 124

TITLES: for different genres, 120; information from, 30–31

TOBY (Wild), 32

TOP STORY, viii

TOPIC SENTENCES, 70; teaching use of, 102

TOPICS: drawing what you know about, 115, 115*f*; explicitly introducing, 100–101; key words lists, 116–117, 116*f*

TRAINING, 82–83

TRAVEL BROCHURE TO ANCIENT GREECE: completed, 106, 107f–108f; explicitly teaching features of, 105–106

TROUBLE: epistemological, 91; interactive, vii, 91, 128; organizational, 91; stylistic, 91

U

UNIT PLANNING MAP, 63, 64f

UNITS: research-based, 113–114, 114t

USING STUDENT ACHIEVEMENT DATA TO IMPROVE STUDENT LEARNING OUTCOMES PROJECT, 81

V

VAN BRAMER, JOAN, 72, 79

VOWEL SOUNDS: read-aloud cloze activity focusing on, 122–123

W

WEEKS, BETTY, ix, 112–125, 127, 130

WESTWOOD, P., vi, x

WHITE, V., 2, 12

WHITE, V.M., 2, 11

WILD, MARGARET, viii, 31–32, 38

WILFRED GORDON MCDONALD PARTRIDGE (FOX): point of view discussion with, 19–20

WILKINSON, LYN, vii, 1–12, 80, 96

WILLSON, P., 50, 60

WIXSON, K., vi, x

WOODCROFT COLLEGE, 97

WORK SAMPLES, 67f, 67–69

WRITING, 3; book responses, 58f, 58–59; Paragraph Planning Sheet, 56, 57f; teaching, 2; *Teddy Magazine*, 46

WRONG ANSWERS, 128

WYATT-SMITH, C.M., 11

Y

YOUNG, S., 2, 12